What people are saying about …

I WANT IT ALL

"Are you looking for more of Jesus in your life? *I Want It All* practically walks you through discovering God's plan in your everyday life. Gwen authentically shares her desires, difficulties, and distractions; however, she doesn't leave you there. You'll learn her battle plan to fight and to fight hard, living victorious each day. Gwen's life experiences provide inspiration and heartfelt truths empowering you to long for more of Jesus, walk daily in His presence and leave a lasting imprint on the lives you influence. *I Want it All* takes you to a new level with Jesus as you discover Him in a fresh way."

Jessie Seneca, More of Him Ministries,
national speaker, and author

"Gwen Smith has powerfully put it all together in one book: the longings, the secret hopes and dreams, the call to believe all we want is possible through Jesus. She is both cheerleader and coach—cheering us on, guiding with the how-to pieces. I want God as a result of reading her words. In that, *I Want It All* is a game changer."

Lisa Whittle, speaker and author
of *Whole* and *I Want God*

I WANT IT ALL

exchanging your average life for **deeper faith, greater power**, and **more impact**

GWEN SMITH

David C Cook®

transforming lives together

I WANT IT ALL
Published by David C Cook
4050 Lee Vance View
Colorado Springs, CO 80918 U.S.A.

David C Cook Distribution Canada
55 Woodslee Avenue, Paris, Ontario, Canada N3L 3E5

David C Cook U.K., Kingsway Communications
Eastbourne, East Sussex BN23 6NT, England

The graphic circle C logo is a registered trademark of David C Cook.

LCCN 2015952821
ISBN 978-0-7814-1370-1
eISBN 978-0-7814-1422-7

© 2016 Gwen Smith
Published in association with William K. Jensen Literary
Agency, 119 Bampton Court, Eugene, OR 97404.

The Team: Ingrid Beck, Liz Heaney, Nick Lee, Tiffany Thomas, Susan Murdock
Cover Design: Amy Konyndyk
Cover Photo: iStockphoto

Printed in the United States of America
First Edition 2016

1 2 3 4 5 6 7 8 9 10

122315

To Preston, Hunter, and Kennedy.
I pray that you will always think
BIG thoughts about God
and live fully immersed in the
grace and truth of Jesus.

CONTENTS

I Want It All

Lord, I want it all today
Every blessing You ordain
Every trial, every strain
Break and build me for Your gain

Humbly now I ask You, lead
Give Your strength where I am weak
Guide each choice and every gaze
Stir my soul to sing Your praise

I want it all, I want Your truth
Bend, correct, inspire, renew
I want the thoughts Your Word instills
To hold and bind me to Your will

So come, Lord, Spirit take control
Help me love You: heart, mind, soul
Pour out treasures, wisdom, peace
In both joy and suffering

Lord, increase my love and faith
Lead me in a dance of grace
Gently shape this lump of clay
To reflect Your glorious name

So bring it on, I want it all
Carve my path: each win, each fall
Every step, please, light my way
'Cause Lord, I want it all today

Gwen Smith

Part 1

ALL THE FAITH

Chapter One

YOURS FOR THE ASKING

I have one desire now—to live a life of reckless abandon for
the Lord, putting all my energy and strength into it.

Elisabeth Elliot, *Through Gates of Splendor*

As I walked into the pink-and-purple bedroom to tuck in my little rose-bud, she sat up in bed and began braiding her hair. She had been waiting for me. News was bubbling in her heart that she simply *had* to share.

Through twists of hair, she began, "Mom! I know what I want to be when I grow up!"

"Well, tell me, Kennedy," I replied, completely smitten with her eight-year-old enthusiasm.

"I want to be a *beautritionist!*"

"A beautritionist?" I questioned, both amused and intrigued.

"Yes, Mom! I want to be a beautritionist!"

"That completely rocks, girlfriend! I'm so excited for you! Do you mean that you want to do hair and makeup and help ladies look beautiful?"

"Yes!"

"Excellent! I think the word you meant to use was *beautician*, but I love the word you made up. The reason I love it is this: you combined two words, *beautician* and *nutritionist*. A beautician helps people look beautiful on the outside by fixing hair and makeup. A nutritionist helps people be healthy and well on the inside. So your new word is awesome, because a beautritionist would help others be healthy on the inside and beautiful on the outside. Yay! Fun! I want to be a beautritionist too, Kennedy!"

We giggled as I tucked her in—snug as a bug in a rug—and prayed for the Lord to help us be the women He created us to be, inside and outside.

Downstairs as I wrote in my journal about the exchange, it occurred to me that Kennedy was really telling me that she has big dreams in her little heart. She wants to make a positive impact on others. To matter. To live days filled with beauty and significance. She wants a life that is the mother lode of greatness.

She wants what we all want.

An incredible life.

We want it all, everything God has for us, but we feel trapped by messy, earthly things. By kids that talk back, jobs that drain us, schedules that leave us stressed, and marriages that are far less than what we had hoped for or expected. We've stopped believing that life is the stuff of little-girl dreams, because way too often, life hurts us. Others fail us. We fail ourselves. We flounder. We disappoint. And let's face it, our failures—our sins—affect our peace and our people ... and often keep us from the best things God has for us.

Reflecting on Kennedy's fledgling desires, I'm forced to be real about the stuffed-down dreams in my own heart. I breathe deep. I'm sobered by the distance between where I am and where I long to be. I really want to be a beautritionist too. I want to rise above average. I want to do more. Be more. Believe deeper. Love better. Worship wholeheartedly. Fly higher.

I find myself wondering how sitting in car-pool lines, going to work, prepping healthy dinners that my family doesn't necessarily appreciate, and hushing sibling squabbles will get me there. I want to be set free from all of these strivings that leave me sucking wind.

It seems as if I'm on a treadmill that doesn't have a STOP button.

I frequently feel like I'm a substandard mom, wife, employee, friend … and Christian. An avalanche of my reality rushes over my heart: I feel overcommitted, ineffective, and distracted. My husband deserves more from me, my kids deserve more, my friends deserve more, my church deserves more, and my God deserves more. I'm tired of being tired.

MORE, PLEASE

I want more.

I want to live beyond ordinary. I want revival. Authentic soul-level revival. I want a maxed-out faith in Jesus that believes big things of God and waits in great expectation for how He is going to show up and show off on Main Street each day.

I want to live a new kind of beauty. One that is deep and mature … far beyond my barely-below-the-surface, suburban soccer-mom tendencies. I want God's grace to trump my grouchy. I want His peace to quiet my anxiousness. I want His plans and power to blow away my small thinking. I want His love to annihilate my indifference, His holiness to consume my sin, His disciplines to prune away my rebellion, and His vision to purify my heart … and purify the world in and through me.

I want it all.

I mean, *I think I do.*

But this kind of *all* seems leaps and bounds more rigorous than the comfortable-ish life I'm used to.

I hesitate. Question.

Do I dare?

Do I dare ask God for *that* kind of all?

MAKE THAT "EVERYTHING"!

If I really want it all—everything God has for me—it's going to be a battle. A beautiful, bloody battle of a girl gone wild for Jesus. A gloves-off, nitty-gritty, leave-it-all-on-the-floor-of-life brawl against a real enemy. A battle where I am in the trenches with a very real, powerful, trustworthy, mysterious, unsafe but faithful God who has promised to never leave my side, to be my defender, to love me beyond my brokenness, to strengthen and guide my weary, stubborn heart, and to work out His plan in and through my life.

Yes.

God has a plan for me, and I do want it. Every part of it. I want to live out God's sacred plan that invites me to a glorious adventure of faith, that beckons me to perfect love, that calls and challenges me to His cross-carrying ways, that demands my everything and satisfies the longings of all I've ever dreamed my life can and should be.

But I promise you, I'm not there yet, and I don't have all the answers. I'm still just a struggling, sojourning sister who fumbles and stumbles countless times each day. I don't write as an authority of all things perfected; I write as one whose will is weak and infiltrated by selfishness, stubbornness, and arrogance.

Allow me to further qualify the journey we're about to embark on together. If you're reading this and feel as if your faith is off-the-charts amazing and you have no struggles, then immediately donate this book to your church library and call it a day. Go get a mani-pedi and sushi with your girlfriends. Email me for a refund. (Kidding.) If, however, you struggle to connect your questions to God's answers, or the harsh realities of your life to God's power, or your choices to God's wisdom, or your apathy to God's calling, then settle in a big, comfy chair. I expect we'll become good friends, and I cannot wait to walk this road with you.

So where are you with all of this "all" business? Are you in? 'Cause I'm chomping at the bit to help lead a band of beautritionists on an all-in adventure to do more believing and less doubting ... to be more courageous and less complacent.

GOD HAS MORE FOR YOU

God has a plan for you too, and it isn't for you to have an "I'm fine," average life.

You were created to be a woman of impact who is so in love with her Lord and so aware of His might that she cannot help but expect great things and move in His power and grace. As D. L. Moody said, "If God is your partner, make your plans big!"

God's plan for you is unique. No cookie-cutter Christianity here.

His plan may not look like the dreams you had as a little girl, but it *is* a good one.

Do you trust that?

God wants you to have a full, beautiful life—in Him, through Him, and for Him. Truly. The Bible tells us so. He offers us joy, but not the world's joy (John 15:11); peace, but not the world's peace (16:33); power, but not the world's power (2 Tim. 1:7); love, but not the world's love (John 15:12–13). God's plan is a good plan ... for us, not against us. A plan that is filled with "hope and a future" (Jer. 29:11). His is a plan that leads us directly to His presence in worship and, ultimately, to a deep and intimate relationship with Him.

And just as God spoke vision and life to the weary prophet Jeremiah thousands of years ago, His Word speaks vision and life to us today, and every day, reminding us of the beauty available to all in Christ. A beauty that brings Him glory.

That's the "all" God wants us to want.

All of Him.

And that's the dream I have for you. That you would read each page of this book and want more of *Him*. That you would groan, grapple, and giggle with me, because even though the struggle is fierce, your faith is growing stronger. My dream is that you would dive deep into the Word and wisdom of God and experience His rest because you have a heart that has been rejuvenated to pursue His power and experience His presence. I want your vision to be expanded, your mind to be blown, and your life to be a compelling display of the love, grace, strength, purity, humility, wisdom, compassion, and mission of Jesus.

This "I want it all" journey will be walked in God's Word and will release you to be the woman God created you to be. Inside and out. It will help you believe and beckon all of the big, bold, bodacious promises of Jesus.

Hear me, friend: those statements aren't some fluffy, rah-rah Christian pep-rally cheers. I know many of you are going through difficult and painful challenges. Life throws curveballs that can leave us gasping for breath on any given day, at any given moment. I'm right there with you in the ditches of reality. God's ways don't always make sense. They don't always feel good. At times they even sting wildly, but one thing is always true: the great life God intends for us to live begins and ends with the Word. The Word made flesh—Jesus. And though we remain broken and impacted by an imperfect world, we can rise above and get through *anything* in the power and hope of God, for His glory.

So, answer this: Are you ready to be a beautritionist? Ready to live the dream? His dream?

Everything God has for you is yours for the asking.

Are you asking?

FOR YOUR REFLECTION AND RESPONSE

- What big dreams did you have as a little girl? What big dreams do you have now? How do the two compare?
- Identify anything in your life that might be keeping you from the best God has for you.
- If you were to ask God for "*that* kind of all," as we talked about in this chapter, how would your life look different from the way you're living now?
- Set a one-sentence goal for your "I want it all" journey. (Tweet your goal to me @GwenSmithMusic using the hashtag #iwantitall or leave a comment on my Facebook wall.)

Chapter Two

THAT THING WE
NEED THE MOST

*It's a bittersweet thing to be really known by someone. All the
rocks you normally hide under have already been overturned.*
Nichole Nordeman, *Love Story*

When my daughter, Kennedy, was four years old, she played on a
peewee soccer team. We signed her up in the hope that she would
have a fun outlet for her overflowing, youthful energy.

On the afternoon of her first practice, I saw great promise. She
was all business as she fearlessly ran down the field and fixed her eyes
and efforts on getting the soccer ball into the goal.

I was stoked! A competitive athlete myself, I envisioned Kennedy
as Mia Hamm junior. Clearly she was about to take peewee soccer to
a whole new level and the Olympic team would soon be sending me
emails about their need for her. I'm sensible like that.

When we got home, Kennedy was elated and exhausted, fully in
love with her new sport. Pride swelled in my mama heart as I gave

my husband the rundown on practice and assured him that we had a very serious four-year-old competitor on our hands. For a week I bragged to family and friends about my little soccer girl and told them of her "Eye of the Tiger" mentality. Shameless, I know.

Thrilled to see his future-Olympian, soccer-playing preschooler in action, my husband, Brad, took Kennedy to her second practice. As they drove off, I waved excitedly, eagerly anticipating a glowing report of her skills and focus upon their return.

When they got home, however, Brad surprised me with his account of what had gone down on and off the field that day. It seems that during this second practice, Kennedy *did not* have a competitive eye of the tiger. Instead, she had a playful desire to catch the eye of her father. All throughout practice—even in the middle of drills—she continually ran to the sidelines, where Brad was watching, to get a drink from her water bottle or to simply give a kiss or get a hug from her daddy. What???

Her eyes were on the prize of another kind: love.

Kennedy delighted in her father's love as she ran to him again and again with arms open wide. She ran to have her thirst quenched in his presence, to express her love, to receive her daddy's tender embrace. She was captivated by love and couldn't resist its draw.

The rewards of soccer were a distant second place to the gold-medal reward of love.

She. Got. It.

She knew that the love of her daddy was the stuff.

The parallel of this wasn't lost on me. God's love is the thing I need most.

There is no other perfect love.

HUNGRY FOR LOVE

I need this truth to impact my thinking and my doing. I wrongly believe that I can live a great life with just a sprinkle of Jesus—just a sip of Living Water—and that the things around me can meet the rest of my longings. I often run around the field of life distracted by the game and glitter of it all instead of running to the ever-so-needed-by-my-soul love of God.

Sadly I'm a bit of a hot mess when it comes to this subject. You see, just like my daughter, I too have an intense desire to be loved. I have ever since I was a kid. I may try to act cucumber cool when it comes to my desperation for love, but don't buy a ticket to that show. It's a farce. Ask my family.

My mom tells a story that when I was a toddler, I used to push my older brother and sister off my dad's lap so I could cuddle with him all by myself. I still do this with my kids and Brad. It might look different today, but my goal is the same: I want more love. And I'm not above pushing someone else out of the way to move myself forward.

My love hunger stumps me. I've been a Christian since I sat on a little plastic Sunday-school chair and learned Bible stories from a flannel-graph board. If I'm so into Jesus—and I promise you, I am—then why am I still needy? Why is my heart such a love vacuum?

I long to be known, adored, and fully accepted.

I may not verbalize it often, but this desire plays on repeat in my internal dialogue.

Anybody else?

The fact of the matter is, I want more love than any human could ever give me. I often look to my husband, children, and friends to fill this ache that churns within me. When will I learn that my people can never fully satiate my longing for more?

I'm so thankful that the Bible reminds me of this intensely personal truth: God is my heavenly Father—my *Abba*—who loves me in the way I've always wanted to be loved. Perfectly. All-sufficiently.

I do want the love of my people. And that's okay. But I can't expect imperfect human beings and relationships to satisfy my heart cravings. Only God can satisfy.

Only God.

GOD'S LOVE IS THE PRIZE

The apostle Paul wrote the book of Ephesians to strengthen and encourage the believers in Ephesus. He wanted the people to "get" the magnitude of God's love and prayed that the Lord would help them experience the reality of it. This is a portion of what Paul wrote:

> I pray that you, being rooted and established in love,
> may have power, together with all the Lord's holy
> people, to grasp how wide and long and high and
> deep is the love of Christ, and to know this love that
> surpasses knowledge—that you may be filled to the
> measure of all the fullness of God. (Eph. 3:17–19)

Paul associated the love of God with power. It's almost as if he was saying, "If you can get this … if you can wrap your head and heart around the truth of just how much God loves you, it will blow you away with blessing. Your faith will pack a punch, and you'll never be the same."

Man! I sure like the sound of that, don't you? Don't you want to be "rooted and established" in God's love? Don't you want your awareness of His love to fill you "to the measure of all the fullness of God"?

Sign me up! I need it. I want it. I want it all.

Check this out. The New Testament part of Scripture was written primarily in Greek. The transliteration of the Greek word for *rooted* that's used in this passage is *rhizoō*, which means "to cause to strike root, to strengthen with roots, to render firm, to fix, establish, cause a person or a thing to be thoroughly grounded." Figuratively it means to "become stable."[1] So my personal summary is this: God's love should stabilize my faith. My acceptance of His love for me will strengthen and "fix" me.

Mind. Blown.

God's love is that thing I need the most. I want that strength. I want that stability. I want every blessing of His love in my life. So I turn to His Word to find out more about this love. And the well is wide, long, high, and deep. Strap on your boots, girlfriend; you're about to be blown away with blessing. You and I will be rooted and established in God's love when we accept the following truths:

- God's love is safe.
- God's love endures.
- God's love satisfies.
- God's love is perfected in us.
- God's love speaks.

By no means is this an exhaustive list. To attempt to fully grasp the love of God would be as ridiculous as trying to contain all the water of Niagara Falls in a teaspoon. Not gonna happen. I will, however, become more firmly rooted and established in God's love for me when I know what the Bible has to say about it. You will too. Let's do this. Let's take a closer look at what each of these truths mean.

GOD'S LOVE IS SAFE

> See what kind of love the Father has given to us,
> that we should be called children of God; and so we
> are. (1 John 3:1 ESV)

When "family" is done right, children are nurtured, cared for, laughed with, encouraged, supported, taught, fed, disciplined, challenged, and protected. They are loved and accepted. Loved—beyond weaknesses, through immaturity and tantrums, in spite of imperfections, with consequences, in word and deed. Accepted—given a place to belong and fit in, given a place to serve, a place to grow, brought into a community.

Yes. We struggle to do this well in a fallen world, but God doesn't. God does family right.

When we place our faith in Jesus, and in our hearts truly believe the gospel—which is to believe that Jesus is the Son of God who came from heaven to earth, lived a perfect life, was crucified to atone for the sins of humanity, was buried and rose again, and is now seated at the right hand of God the Father in heaven—the Bible says that we're adopted into God's family. God takes us in as His own. And God takes family seriously.

I realize that *family* isn't a safe word for everybody, but it should be. The family of God is a place of safety (minus the human factor that messes it up). God shows us His love when He calls us His children. I am a child of God. I am also a mom. I love my kids so much it hurts. I would stand in front of a speeding train to keep them safe. Yet God's love dwarfs my mama love. By calling me His child, God makes an intimate and powerful declaration that I belong to Him.

I am His. He is mine.

You are His. He is yours.

Forever.

GOD'S LOVE ENDURES

This leads me to the next truth—it is eternal. Knowing this helps me a lot. It makes me feel secure. Earthly love can be fickle, frail, temporary, and disappointing. Spouses abandon their marriages and families. Parents turn their backs on their children. Children turn their backs on their families. Friendships dissolve and change from season to season and city to city. But God's love never changes. His love is steadfast. It remains. It is unbreakable. Never ending. Unlike the love I experience with people, the Lord's love will never diminish. The apostle Paul painted a picture of the never-ending, can't-be-stopped love of God in his letter to the Roman believers:

> In all these things we are more than conquerors
> through him who loved us. For I am sure that nei-
> ther death nor life, nor angels nor rulers, nor things
> present nor things to come, nor powers, nor height

nor depth, nor anything else in all creation, will be
able to separate us from the love of God in Christ
Jesus our Lord. (Rom. 8:37–39 ESV)

And because the Bible says I can always count on God's love to
be there for me, I relax a bit. The struggles of the world seem less
daunting because I know I'm God's daughter and He's got my back.

GOD'S LOVE SATISFIES

Another biblical truth about God's love that digs my faith deep is
that it satisfies. I know I already told you how needy I am when it
comes to love, but let me revisit my pathetic desperation. Remember
that game Hungry Hungry Hippos? Well, I'm pretty much Hungry
Hungry Gwenno. (Don't remember that game? Google it and then
buy it for your four-year-old nephew, neighbor, or grandkid. You'll
thank me.)

It seems our old friend Moses was a bit of a hungry hippo too.
In Psalm 90 he asked God to fill him and God's people full of love:
"Satisfy us in the morning with your unfailing love, that we may sing
for joy and be glad all our days" (v. 14). Love this! Note that Moses
connected the love of God with a satisfaction that put a song in his
heart and a skip in his step.

Yes. I want this too. So my prayer each morning becomes, *Satisfy
me with Your love today, Lord. Fill me with Your joy and gladness, and
lead my actions to sing of You.*

As I pray this, His companionship meets my loneliness.

His grace overwhelms my grump.

His joy trumps my anger.

His provision satisfies my need.

David recognized that he needed God's all-satisfying love too. He celebrated it … was desperate for it … was responsive to it. Look at what he penned in the familiar words of Psalm 63:

> You, God, are my God,
>> earnestly I seek you;
> I thirst for you,
>> my whole being longs for you,
> in a dry and parched land
>> where there is no water.
>
> I have seen you in the sanctuary
>> and beheld your power and your glory.
> Because your love is better than life,
>> my lips will glorify you.
> I will praise you as long as I live,
>> and in your name I will lift up my hands.
> I will be fully satisfied as with the richest of foods;
>> with singing lips my mouth will praise you.
>> (vv. 1–5)

I see my own heart reflected in David's words and realize that when I'm hankering for a hunk of love, my longings are best met in the arms of my Lord. His is the love of power and glory. His love is "better than life." And, like David, I choose to respond to His love with worship. My lips will glorify Him. I will lift up my hands. I will praise the all-worthy One. In doing so, my soul is secure. Satisfied.

Ultimately I experience the satisfaction of God's love through Jesus. God's perfect love compelled Him to sacrifice His Son to bridge the chasm of death between His holiness and my humanness. His is the love that holds, the love that heals, the love that refines, the love that calls my waywardness back to purity with kindness, the love that is always with me, that rejoices over me with singing and takes "great delight" in me (Zeph. 3:17).

This sacred, scarlet love of Jesus is the only water that can quench the desperate longings of my thirsty soul. If I want all the love God has for me, my feeble hands must reach for the ones that were pierced for my transgressions. Every day. When the sun shines. When the storm screams. I find God's love when I reach out to Jesus.

His is the only love that satisfies.

GOD'S LOVE IS PERFECTED IN US

The apostle John had this to say about the love of God:

> In this the love of God was made manifest among us, that God sent his only Son into the world, so that we might live through him. In this is love, not that we have loved God but that he loved us and sent his Son to be the propitiation for our sins. Beloved, if God so loved us, we also ought to love one another. No one has ever seen God; if we love

one another, God abides in us and *his love is per-fected in us.* (1 John 4:9–12 ESV)

His love … perfected in us?

Yes, please.

Lord, perfect Your love in me.

Later on, in the "All the Impact" section of this book, we'll talk about what it looks like to mobilize God's love. What I think we need to grasp here is that God's love is foundational to our faith. It's essential. In our humanness, our love is grossly inadequate, but when God allows His divine love to flow through us, it is beautiful and sufficient. Jesus said the love that believers show one another gives evidence to the world of our discipleship (John 13:34–35). Makes me wonder. Am I loving other Christians in a way that shows the nonbelieving world that I'm a follower of Christ?

For God's love to be perfected in me, confession is a must. The good news is that God is all about renewal, a good refreshing. His Word says that when I confess my sins, God will forgive them and purify my heart (1 John 1:9). No ifs, ands, or buts about it. By faith I must believe it. Then I move forward in His love and let it move forward in me.

The author of Hebrews encouraged New Testament believers in a similar way: "Let us throw off everything that hinders and the sin that so easily entangles. And let us run with perseverance the race marked out for us, fixing our eyes on Jesus, the pioneer and perfecter of faith" (12:1–2). Jesus is the author and perfecter of my faith. When I yield my life to Him by humbly confessing my mistakes and shortcomings, when I abide in Him and love others, His love is mysteriously perfected in me.

GOD'S LOVE SPEAKS

There are so many layers to God's love. It *really* is the prize. Not only is His love safe, enduring, satisfying, and perfected in me through Christ, but God's love also speaks. It is a continuous conversation—interactive and personal. Because of this, I have a constant Companion. In times when I feel alone, I actually never am. This comforts me. God is attentive to me in His divinely inspired love letter. The Bible is a timeless note that expresses His interest in me.

And let me tell you, I love a good note.

When I was in high school in the late 1980s, the halls buzzed with everything you would expect, including note passing. When you got a note, you didn't just let it hang out in the pockets of your Calvin Kleins or shove it in your leg warmers; you took it out and devoured it. And then you wrote back, circling *yes* or *no* to the questions. *Do you like him? Did you watch* 21 Jump Street *last night? Did you kiss him? Are you going to Kelly's birthday party? Have you heard the latest song by Tears for Fears? Will you go with me?*

Notes were a dialogue. They helped you connect with friends, scope out possible love interests, break up, make up, and everything in between. Rarely was just one note passed between two people. (And rarely were teachers happy about them.)

Get this: God made sure that we got a note from Him. A love note to pursue our hearts and connect our hearts to His. A personal note that is addressed to each of us and ends with "Love, God." His love is poured out chapter by chapter, verse by verse, all so we might understand and accept that His intentions for us are as unique as a snowflake and as extravagant as an ocean sunset.

When I'm feeling unappreciated, unimportant, or rejected, it helps to remember that God's love speaks. I need only listen. Your days may sting with an unfulfilled longing, a perceived inadequacy, a devastating loss, or a gaping heart wound. Might I offer a word of encouragement? Whether you're a mother, a grandmother, a sister, or a daughter; whether you're single, married, widowed, or divorced; whether your loved ones value and cherish you or wound you with broken behavior, God loves you, knows you, and cherishes you *perfectly*. Let His love speak life to you.

The Lord declared to Israel, "I have loved you, my people, with an everlasting love. With unfailing love I have drawn you to myself" (Jer. 31:3 NLT). Just as He spoke these words to His children, the Israelites, long ago, God speaks across the universe today to each daughter's heart: "I notice you!" "You are special to Me." "You matter." "I love you ... perfectly ... eternally ... completely, and I really, really, really mean it."

He showed us His love through the death and resurrection of His Son, Jesus.

His Spirit whispers that love to the hearts of His children continuously.

He speaks it through His Word.

Are you listening?

Once you open and read God's love note, you'll want to respond. To go back and forth in conversation, deepening the relationship. To circle yes or no to His questions: "Do you know how much I love you? Are you aware of the distance between My holiness and your sin? Will you let My love meet you in your achy places? Will you ask for My help with that decision? Do you know how beautiful you are to Me? Will you move beyond lukewarm living today, fight through your indifference, and become freshly astonished by My grace? Will you trust Me with that roadblock? Will you acknowledge Me as the source of your significance and the validation you are desperate for?"

I want my answers to be yes. I want to be so deeply rooted and grounded in God's love that it stabilizes my faith, no matter how unstable the other factors of my life seem. Don't you? I've said it before and I'll say it again: the true reward of God's love is found in Jesus Christ.

EYES ON THE PRIZE

When we focus our gaze on perfect Love, you and I can confidently say, "I want it all, all the love God has for me. I want a sacred awareness that shatters my indifference. I want a raging revival deep within to drive the temperature of my faith beyond lukewarm. I want to hear every whisper that the Word speaks to my heart. And I want to embrace my loving heavenly Father, who is patient, kind, full of compassion, slow to anger, and deeply in love with me."

I want all of Him.

Every ounce of the Love that never fails.

Every ounce of Jesus.

Yes, I want it all.

FOR YOUR REFLECTION AND RESPONSE

- When your soul is thirsty, where do you run for refreshment?
- Which of the biblical truths about God's love talked about in this chapter spoke most to you? Why?
- One of the God questions in this chapter reads, "Will you move beyond lukewarm living today, fight through your indifference, and become freshly astonished by My grace?" What *is* your indifference?
- What can you do today to help keep your eyes on the prize?

Chapter Three

NOT JUST A PRAYER WE SAY BEFORE DINNER

Grace goes beyond mercy. Mercy gave the prodigal son a second chance. Grace threw him a party. Mercy prompted the Samaritan to bandage the wounds of the victim. Grace prompted him to leave his credit card as payment for the victim's care. Mercy forgave the thief on the cross. Grace escorted him into paradise.

Max Lucado, *Wild Grace*

I had been playing with my dad's stopwatch that had been carefully placed on his desk, away from the reach of children. He was a track coach for the high school where he worked. Track coaches needed stopwatches, and they were pretty pricey back in the day.

Clumsy since the minute of my birth, I broke the stopwatch. Panic consumed my heart. Then I hid the damaged timepiece in hopes that Dad would never know what I had done. Yeah, I'm optimistic that way.

My neighbor Kate and I were hanging out a few days later at her house. I remember it well. "Stairway to Heaven" wafted from

the record player in her older sister's room. She had just bought
the LP and spun it continuously. It was the early eighties. Since I
was a good church girl, I was certain that if we went upstairs and
played that album backward, we would hear a creepy message from
the Devil.

"Gwen, your dad's on the phone!" Mrs. Sloane called out from
the kitchen.

"Hey, Dad! What's up?" I asked as I grabbed the phone.

"Hi, Gwen. Were you playing with my stopwatch? I just found it
on my desk, and it's broken. I've asked the other kids, and they said
that it wasn't them. That leaves you."

Stomach flops.

"I'm sorry, Daddy! It was an accident. I didn't mean to break it.
I'm really sorry."

Lump in throat.

"You need to come home so we can discuss this. I'll see you in a
few minutes. Bye."

Click.

My blood ran cold, and fear gripped me. I ran the whole way
across two yards to our house, horrified that I would be grounded
until the day I wore a wedding gown. If I even lived to wear one!

As it turns out, my dad was more upset with the hiding than
he was with the breaking. There were consequences. And there was
forgiveness. Then it was over. I don't know that we ever even talked
about it after my punishment was completed and his grace had been
given. What was broken and hidden became healed and forgiven
when my father gifted me with grace.

I want ... I need ... I cherish grace.

UNCOMFORTABLE, MESSY, GREATER-THAN GRACE

Grace. It's not just a prayer we say before a meal. Grace is something we experience. A gift we give and receive that is neither shallow nor simple nor one sentence long. It's deep, complicated, costly, beautiful, and eternal. Far from neat and proper, it is messy inside out and upside down. Grace is uncomfortable. After all, it just doesn't seem right that I can be forgiven and set free from my failures and rebellions.

Jesus is the apex of grace. He is the perfecting point of connection between our fallen humanity and God's divine forgiveness.

Jesus. Fully man. Fully God. My source of grace.

As for me, I'm just a train wreck of a woman. Fully flawed: arrogant, stubborn, and vibrantly aware of the shortcomings that shout my depravity. But meaningfully changed, to the core, by His grace that is greater than.

Greater than my junky attitudes.

Greater than my biases and pride.

Greater than my wounds and struggles.

Greater than my wandering ways.

Greater than my limitations and weaknesses.

I'm in desperate need of Jesus and His grace. But hear me clearly. I need the Jesus of the Bible, not the white, fiscally conservative, Republican Jesus that many of us church peeps like to make Him out to be. And not the white or black, socialist-progressive, democratic, social justice, liberation theology Jesus that many others make Him out to be. (Yes. I just went there.)

I need more of the *real* Jesus in my life.

The Jesus who had compassion on everyone He encountered, compassion that didn't depend on whether that person knew Him, looked like Him, served Him, or led a pure life.

The Jesus who touched the untouchables, fed the hungry, and saw the unseen.

I need more of the grace-on-a-mission-to-make-what-is-unholy-holy Jesus. I need more of the One who spoke to those society said He should ignore and think of as less than. The Jesus who condemned the prideful religious people with all their legalism and answers … and instead hung out with tree-climbing lawbreakers who were full of questions and curiosity but were ready to humbly follow Him. The One who *gave* far more than He got and *loved* far more than He was loved.

We Christians often worry about the rights and wrongs of other people more than we worry about our own sins. We spend three hours a day listening to talk radio or watching a cable news channel and spend three minutes in prayer. We judge the homeless man with the cardboard sign and are convinced he's probably going to spend our hard-earned five dollars on alcohol, so we choose not to be generous. We choose not to help. We choose not to glance too long at people who require a great deal of our time, our efforts, or our money. After all, it's ours. Right?

Oh how it must cause God's heart to ache for us to take, take, take of His grace but be stingy with it when it comes to other people.

Is this too bold? Am I being over-the-top intense here? I wonder as I write. My next thought: *Good glory, I hope so!* Because I need to live with a greater-than grace that is intentional to the point that it makes me uncomfortable.

I need all of the grace of Jesus! I do. I do. I do.

I need it.

But do I really *want* it all?

After all, part of what makes grace so messy and uncomfortable is that it often goes into the dark back alleys of our lives where we try to hide our sin.

GRACE PURSUES THE HIDDEN

We see this in the story of the woman in John 4. Jesus was tired and stopped to rest at Jacob's well where He began a conversation with a Samaritan woman, ignoring the cultural, racial, and social norms of the day. (Jews did not associate with Samaritans and often tried to avoid Samaria altogether on their journeys. In addition to that, respectable Jewish men did not talk to women they didn't know.) But Jesus wasn't concerned about public opinion. He was on a mission of mercy.

Her name is never mentioned, but He knew it.

He knew not only her name but her insecurities, her reputation, her fears, her failures, and her needs.

Jesus asked this unnamed woman for a drink and then engaged her in a meaningful and purposeful conversation. They talked of practical thirst; then Jesus spoke of living water that satisfies eternally.

Not realizing who in the world she was talking to or what He was really chatting about, this woman asked for a full-to-the-tippy-top jar of living water so she would never be thirsty again. "Show me the money, Jewish man. I want some of that water because I am *so* over making these constant trips to the well." (Bless her! I mean, who wouldn't want that? I get this woman. If I never had to buy groceries again, I'd be one happy girl!)

Then to lovingly introduce this thirsty girl to the Living Water she longed for, Jesus redirected the conversation, asking her to go call her husband and then come back (v. 16). Why? Because she didn't have a husband, and He knew it. She'd had lover after lover.

> "I have no husband," she replied.
>
> Jesus said to her, "You are right when you say you have no husband. The fact is, you have had five husbands, and the man you now have is not your husband. What you have just said is quite true." (vv. 17–18)

Dang! He called her out. As light invades darkness, this conversation instantly went from veiled and casual to exposed and personal. I imagine that she squirmed like crazy under her covering as she acknowledged that this man must be a prophet. Uncomfortable, she tried to change the subject by talking about religion instead of her rebellion. She told him,

> "Our ancestors worshiped on this mountain, but you Jews claim that the place where we must worship is in Jerusalem."
>
> "Woman," Jesus replied, "believe me, a time is coming when you will worship the Father neither on this mountain nor in Jerusalem. You Samaritans worship what you do not know; we worship what

we do know, for salvation is from the Jews. Yet a
time is coming and has now come when the true
worshipers will worship the Father in the Spirit and
in truth, for they are the kind of worshipers the
Father seeks. God is spirit, and his worshipers must
worship in the Spirit and in truth." (vv. 19–24)

What did Jesus mean by saying we must worship God in *truth*?
The root word for *truth* in this verse is *alēthia*, which means "hiding
nothing."[1] So to worship God in truth means that we are to come
before Him hiding nothing. It means that we must bare all to the
One who sees and knows all. It means that we should come as we are,
allowing our stained hearts to be made white as snow in the presence
of our holy God, who dwells in unapproachable light.

Friend, God isn't looking for us to be religious, and He certainly
knows all about the rebellion we try to hide. He knows when you
flirt with that married man at work or with an old boyfriend on
Facebook. He knows when you're sexually intimate with that boyfriend. He knows when you secretly put away shopping bags and
throw away receipts before your husband gets home. He knows when
you surrender to eating that entire bag of potato chips, when you
cut yourself to anesthetize the pain, when you make yourself throw
up after meals. He knows about that affair. He knows when gossip
dances on your lips and when your heart hangs on to unforgiveness,
jealousy, anger, deceit, hatred, and ugliness.

He knows it *all*, and in His knowing, He invites you to bring
what is hidden into the light so that you can experience His restoring
grace. I know because that is exactly what He did for me.

GRACE HEALS AND RESTORES

Fair warning: My story is about to avalanche into a disastrous mess here. Trying to sanitize it would only serve to keep me from embarrassment and protect my pride. I know that I'm not defined by my failures, and I refuse to minimize the grace of God that deserves to be maximized. So I will share—the good, the bad, and the ugly.

Deep breath.

I went off to college with big dreams and great expectations of what God and I would accomplish together. I had grown in faith over the years and was in love with Jesus. Convinced that God's plans were best for me, I was a college freshman who sought His leading, stayed in the Word, and sang along with Steven Curtis Chapman when he belted out, "We will abandon it all for the sake of the call."

Until I didn't.

Until I didn't abandon it all—all that the world offered.

Instead, I abandoned the will of God.

College was different. There were so many choices. In the cafeteria I could eat french fries and dessert with every meal if I wanted to. Mom didn't put veggies on my dinner plate and expect me to eat them anymore. Fabulous. In the dorm there was no curfew. I could come and go as I pleased. In the classroom, no roll calls. The freedom was intoxicating, and the allure of compromise was powerful.

And I caved.

Gradually and subtly I caved.

I didn't start hating on Jesus or anything. I just didn't find Him or the ways of the Bible as compelling as my other options. I still went to church, but in my heart I set God's will aside for a season ... and I wanted Him to keep quiet about it.

One foot in. One foot out. I played the Hokey Pokey with God.

I didn't need to follow *all* of His commands, did I? I mean, c'mon. His guidelines made partying way less exciting. And sin can seem very fun, you know. For a season.

Regretfully, I had to find out the hard way that sin is always tied with a death rope—and I hung myself with it my junior year.

Shacking up was the thing in college. When you dated a guy, you slept with him.

Even church girls did it.

I only slept with that one guy. The one I was dating and fell in love with. The one who also loved Jesus and went to campus ministry meetings with me.

You read that right.

I thought I was *living the life* until everything spiraled out of control when I got pregnant my junior year, chose death for my child in an abortion clinic, and then fell into a deep pit of darkness.

Then I hid. And trembled.

In the darkness. In the death. In my shame. In my horror.

Light had no place there.

I was confident that I could never be healed or whole or well again.

I didn't even want to be well. It was too good for me. I deserved darkness and pain and all the tears and regret that ravaged my heart.

I deserved death, since I chose it for my baby.

Sin wasn't shiny anymore.

It was tar. Mucky. Sticky. Dark. Thick. Hot. Painful.

Sin closes hearts. And a closed heart isn't easy to pry open. Mine was closed. Locked and bolted. And devastated.

Until the knocks came.

The persistent, uninvited knocks on the door of my heart.

"Where are you, Gwen? Come back!"

I heard Grace pursuing me. Mercy whispered through conversations, sermons, and directly to my heart when I was still.

I covered my ears. I could never turn back to Jesus. I had wandered too far. Done too much. Forgiveness was for everyone else. Not for me. It could never be for me.

The gift was too massive. The light of it too bright. Utterly and completely undeserved.

But Grace heard the cries my heart refused to express and pursued me in the pit. Grace doesn't play by the rules of fairness. In spite of me, in spite of my defiance, Grace became my defense when Jesus invaded the darkness of my failings and stood between me and my sin.

Confessions fell from my heart like rain in a torrential storm. I was undone, wrung out, revived, and rebuilt by forgiveness. By Grace. By Jesus.

Then peace filled my soul as God lifted me from the dark pit, set my feet on a rock, and put a new song in my heart. He forgave this woman whose womb had been emptied by abortion and filled her with a burden to protect and cherish life. What was broken and hidden became healed and forgiven when my Father restored me with grace.

Darkness into light.

Turmoil into tranquillity.

Broken into beautiful.

Grace. Changes. Everything.

God is all about healing wounded hearts. His grace empowers me to embrace both the good and the grit of my past and present ... because God can make all things—every last experience and circumstance—work together for my good if I love Him and trust His sovereignty (Rom. 8:28). Even my abortion.

The psalmist tells us, "He [God] heals the brokenhearted and binds up their wounds" (Ps. 147:3). The word *heals* in this verse is the Hebrew word *rapha*,[2] which means "to mend, to repair, to cure, to purify, to rebuild, to make whole." We regret, we blame, we hide, we bleed, we shame ourselves and walk around wounded. From church lobby to church lobby. Pew to pew. These feelings seem right, but they eat us up from the inside out.

God wants to heal our wounds. He gives us what we don't deserve when He rebuilds our lives in grace ... when He cures our sin problem with forgiveness ... when He makes our broken hearts whole again. But for us to experience this healing, we must accept this truth and allow grace to heal our heart wounds.

Have you allowed God to heal your heart wounds? I have. And after my wounded heart was healed, I began to realize that grace isn't just for my past mistakes; it's for my present and future mistakes too.

WORKING OUT THE KINKS

By faith we believe that God's grace has covered the shame of our yesterdays, but what about this morning's failure? What's a girl to do with that? Perhaps a metaphor will help.

As of last summer, I became a watering girl. My sunny days often begin with a garden hose in hand. And I love it. The birds sing melodies in all their chirpy cuteness, and the plants respond with claps of gratitude. (I seriously think they clap … in their own way. Moving on …)

Early one morning I unwound the hose and watered our small cucumber garden. Then I headed toward a few thirsty plant friends in the back of the lawn along the fence. As I began to water, the flow trickled to a stop.

I looked up and spied the water-stopping nemesis. A kink in the hose.

So frustrating.

There was plenty of water. It just couldn't flow because the hose had flipped and kinked. I tried to flap it out from where I was across the yard, but this kink was a good bit down the line. It required that I drop everything and address it. Once the kink was fixed, the water flowed smoothly, and the rest of my plants got their drinks.

What a picture of faith!

Just as a hose is connected to a water source, our souls are connected to the Living Water. And although as believers we're always connected to Him and always have access to the refreshment and nourishment our souls need, there are times when kinks happen and the flow stops.

My kinks come in all shapes and sizes. I get flipped over by disappointments, unmet expectations, other people, or simply by my attitudes, unbelief, fears, behaviors, rebellion, or unhealthy emotions.

How can I work out the kinks of my circumstances and relationships? By turning to the grace that God offers. By asking for His grace instead of depending on my own strength. By going to Him in prayer. By aligning my life and my choices to the teachings of the Bible. By yielding to His Spirit.

The biggest of all kinks, however, is my sin.

Yep. I said the s word.

Pastor Timothy Keller said it this way: "The sin that is most destructive in your life right now is the one you are most defensive about."[3]

Ouch. Big kink. Right?

How can I work out the kinks of my sin? By confession. I drop everything and address it. Here are two opposite sides of the same kink coin found in Scripture:

> If we say we have no sin, we deceive ourselves, and the truth is not in us. If we confess our sins, he is faithful and just to forgive us our sins and to cleanse us from all unrighteousness. If we say we have not sinned, we make him a liar, and his word is not in us. (1 John 1:8–10 ESV)

> If anyone, then, knows the good they ought to do and doesn't do it, it is sin for them. (James 4:17)

Got a few sin kinks? Sure you do. We all do. Some might stem from blatant rebellion against God's will, while others might be simply *not* doing something you know you ought to do. Regardless, if you want to have a right relationship with God, you must deal with sin honestly. Nothing can separate you from God's love (Rom. 8:39), but sin sure can stop the flow of His peace, grace, strength, and joy into your life.

The Anglican theologian Richard Sibbes summed up the good news of Jesus beautifully when he said, "There is more mercy in Christ than sin in us."[4]

I. Am. So. Thankful.

Let the grace of God work out your kinks as they happen. When you realize your error, drop everything and address it. The Bible says that the Lord's kindness leads us to repentance (Rom. 2:4), which, in turn, unleashes the powerful flow of His peace, grace, strength, and joy.

Now I admit this isn't always easy. There are times when I want to justify my sin and ignore grace. But if I can recognize my stubbornness, pride, arrogance, laziness, overindulgence, and so on for what they are and remember that God's grace restores and heals, I'll be empowered to handle my sin swiftly and sincerely.

LIVING IN THE POWER OF GOD'S GRACE

Mind if we unkink a few more hoses? This is a biggie. Whenever I share my story of how the grace of God restored me from the ruins of my abortion and talk about the freedom I have because of the forgiveness of Christ, I usually get "The Question."

Sometimes the asker leans forward to inquire while I sign the book or CD she just bought. Sometimes she grips my hands and whispers that "we have the same story" and *then* asks The Question. Sometimes she waits until everyone else has gone home before she allows it to leave her lips. Regardless of the delivery method, I get asked The Question all the time: "How were you able to forgive yourself?"

And then it's usually followed up with this doozy: *I know that the Bible says that God forgives me if I confess my sin, but I just can't forgive myself.*

This might be your struggle. If so, please pay close attention to this truth. I am free and forgiven because of Jesus, not because of me. When I say that grace changes everything, I mean *everything.* The Bible says so!

Can I be a velvet hammer for a minute here and speak directly?

This "I can't forgive myself" jargon bears no weight biblically. Your sin isn't the exception to God's willingness to forgive. You haven't found a loophole. If you "can't" forgive yourself (or another person), then at least be honest with yourself and recognize that your choice—yes, I said choice—to not forgive is outside the scope of God's will. Period.

Do you want to live in the power of God's grace? Do you want to grow in faith and experience the Spirit of God at work within you? (You whispered yes, right?) Good. Then you have to choose to forgive yourself. (Or him. Or her. Or them.) Because living in God's grace requires that you forgive others and that you forgive yourself.

Jesus Himself said, "If you forgive other people when they sin against you, your heavenly Father will also forgive you. But if you do not forgive others their sins, your Father will not forgive your sins" (Matt. 6:14–15). God's plan of grace is for your restoration … for your healing … for your freedom. "So if the Son sets you free, you will be free indeed" (John 8:36).

Be. Free. In. Christ.

His grace is enough. And it will lead you to so much more.

GRACE RESTARTS YOUR MORE

Jesus took on death so you and I could take on life. A life of more.

The more we're meant for isn't found in an empty bottle, a full womb, or a man's arms. It isn't found in a clean medical chart or in that promotion at work. It isn't found in a home that shows like an HGTV showcase or in well-behaved children. It's found in Jesus Christ.

God's grace invites us to a restart that begins with repentance and grows our faith. When we decide to follow Christ, the *more* begins. His more.

Jesus calls us to a vulnerable, honest faith.

When the Samaritan woman met Jesus at Jacob's well, she was changed by grace (John 4). She had gone to the well around midday, all alone, as an outcast who lived in the shadows of shame, sin, and isolation. She left as a changed woman who ran to tell her community about Jesus. Many in the town placed their faith in Christ as a result of her testimony (v. 39). Grace redirected her to the more God had for her. Grace led her from lonely living into a community of believers and allowed a rebellious female to become a redemptive force for good.

Jesus asks all of us to worship Him in humble awareness of our sinfulness and with a sacred awareness of His grace that connects us to forgiveness, restoration, healing, peace, hope, joy, and unfailing love. These are the things I want to be connected to!

And I am.

While I used to live with the shame and secrets of promiscuity and abortion, I am now free. And the grace of God leads me to the *more* He has for me each time I share about the forgiveness I have in Christ. My life has been transformed. The very things that made me hide from the world have been turned upside down and have become a tool of hope for other women.

And with that bit of awesomeness, we end our discussion on grace. As I think through these promises, my faith grows. I realize that the simplified message of grace is that God wants to impact my past, present, and future with restoration, healing, and His *more*. Instead of pretending that everything is fine, I now nip my kinks in the bud and confess what needs confessing. I'm thankful that God's grace leads me to a stronger faith. And I live to be free in Christ because I am *so* done wading in the shallow end of the grace pool. How about you?

FOR YOUR REFLECTION AND RESPONSE

- What exchange do we accept when our view of grace is comfortable and shallow?
- If you had a private conversation with Jesus that went from casual to personal, what would He call you out on?
- What would it look like for you to worship God hiding nothing?
- What sin are you most defensive about?
- What are some of the kinks in your hose?
- Ready to move forward in your *more* with Jesus? If so, find me on Twitter, add me, and let me know! (Tweet "I am ready for more!" to me @GwenSmithMusic using the hashtag #iwantitall or leave a comment on my Facebook wall.)

Chapter Four

CAN YOU REALLY HUG A PORCUPINE?

Hope doesn't announce that life is safe, therefore, we will be; instead,
it whispers that Christ is our safety in the midst of harsh reality.

Patsy Clairmont, *Dancing Bones*

My friend Dave gives great advice. He isn't just a friend; he's a mentor, and he helps me grow both professionally and personally. Years ago Dave taught me to pay attention to what moves me emotionally. To hang out there awhile. To be present and in the moment. To consider what it is that triggers me toward a response. He says that this awareness leads us to create honest, compelling, and meaningful art. I agree.

One of the church anthems of today that moves me every time is a song by Hillsong United called "Oceans." The allure of this song is not just melodic, although the melody is exquisite. Depth of beauty is found in the lyrics because of their complexity and raw vulnerability. To sing it from the heart is dangerous because it requires that a worshipper surrender the scariest, darkest places of her life to God. It compels her to trust without borders, with no limits. To take a free fall of faith.

The presence of God is powerful when we face intimidating circumstances. In Isaiah 43, the Lord spoke to His chosen ones, the Israelites, of His commitment to be their rescue:

> This is what the LORD says—
>> he who created you, Jacob,
>> he who formed you, Israel:
> "Do not fear, for I have redeemed you;
>> I have summoned you by name; you are mine.
> When you pass through the waters,
>> I will be with you;
> and when you pass through the rivers,
>> they will not sweep over you.
> When you walk through the fire,
>> you will not be burned;
>> the flames will not set you ablaze.
> For I am the LORD your God,
>> the Holy One of Israel, your Savior." (vv. 1–3)

We tremble. God says, "Do not fear."

We wander. Grace calls out to us by name.

We wane in the heat of firestorms. Love shields us from the flames.

We struggle in the streams and are swayed by the currents. God reaches for shaky hands, grips us with comfort, and assures us that we are not alone.

He holds on tight and keeps our heads above the water.

I know this in my heart. I know this is true. I know His presence is real and His rescues are promised, but when the waves keep crashing on the shore one after another, I find myself exhausted from the strain ... and I wonder if God might have taken a day off. Like maybe He went to Cabo and is sipping an umbrella drink on a beach resort somewhere. It's not as if He doesn't deserve a break, you know! He does so much for so many.

But no! I know better.

God doesn't even take naps. Only my faith does.

Wake up, sleepy soul. Wake up!

In order for you and me to have a faith so strong it can withstand whatever life brings our way—the hurricanes, cancer treatments, eating disorders, hard conversations with hardened hearts, joblessness, broken relationships, doubts that seek to drown us—our hands must raise in surrender to the things He allows. And our eyes must constantly search for His.

If I want all the faith God has for me, I have to want all the depth, all the growth, all the profundity that comes from knowing Jesus. I need to want maturity and intimacy with Him more than I want comfort. And when God calls me out into the deep waters of a trial, I want to be a woman who doesn't run.

HUGS AND HURTS

Several years ago I bought a box of Cheerios that came with a free children's book. I love free stuff—especially when said freebie comes with an item I would buy regardless. The little book that came with the *o*'s had a darling and oh-so-prickly little varmint on the front cover. The title? *How Do You Hug a Porcupine?*[1]

The story is about a young boy who witnessed several of his friends hugging a myriad of animals. They hugged dogs, bunnies, cats, horses, cows—you get the picture … all cuddly and relatively safe. All the while, the young boy was wondering how he could hug a porcupine. Why? I'm not sure. It's a children's book. Go with it. The main character tried several creative ways to approach his quilled friend. He didn't want to get hurt, so at first he donned some base-ball catcher's gear; then he tried reaching from far away while a box protected his body, and finally he attempted to tame the spikes with marshmallows. By the end of the book, he concluded that he needed to move slowly, and the best way to hug a porcupine is this: *carefully.*

Cute story. Simple ending. I just wish that hugging the porcu-pines in my life could be such a simple and cute adventure.

We all have them, you know … porcupines. Struggles, trials, pains, mountains, call them what you will; they exist and they are prickly. And strangely, *oh so strangely*, the Bible tells us that we are supposed to hug them.

Seriously? Yep.

Here it is in black and white:

> Consider it pure joy, my brothers and sisters, whenever you face trials of many kinds, because you know that the testing of your faith produces perseverance. Let perseverance finish its work so that you may be mature and complete, not lacking anything. (James 1:2–4)

The Message sums it up this way:

> Consider it a sheer gift, friends, when tests and challenges come at you from all sides. You know that under pressure, your faith-life is forced into the open and shows its true colors. So don't try to get out of anything prematurely. Let it do its work so you become mature and well-developed, not deficient in any way.

Now, let me just go ahead and ask the questions we all wonder. How in the world are we supposed to think of tests and challenges as *gifts*—as pure *joy*? I've read this charge a million times, yet the tension of it still grinds me like fingernails on a chalkboard. I mean, c'mon! It's insanity to consider it pure joy when we suffer and go through hard things.

When I'm going through a tough time, my natural response is to complain or feel sorry for myself, not to say, "Thanks for the gift, Lord! Oh, what joy!" And if this is a *good* thing for me—to embrace my struggles—then why is there such a disconnect between my warm longings and this cold calling?

I look around at the groanings of humankind and wonder if God can truly be loving *and* allow little girls to be molested by loved ones … porn-addicted husbands to walk out or shut down … racists to gun down innocent believers at a Bible study … natural disasters to wreak havoc on civilization as they wipe out beating hearts by the thousands … millions of preborn babies to be legally slaughtered in the name of women's rights.

The simple answer is: Yes. He can.

But what He allows in His sovereignty is far from simple.

Far from neat.

Far from understandable.

So how is it that the Bible teaches that for us to embrace all God has for us, we have to count the trials of our lives as blessings?

I see you squirming. *I don't like this conversation, Gwen! Why can't we just talk about the comfortable side of Christianity, like love, grace, peace, unity, potluck dinners, unspoken prayer requests, and heaven? Where's the Easy Button?*

Not here.

Not in this chapter.

And certainly not in our Christian calling.

While a life purposed for Christ is chock-full of blessings—many of which *are* completely incredible and comfortable—each surrendered life is also filled with struggles that God uses to help us become mature and complete. The Bible doesn't sugarcoat this. It says that we are *promised* challenges and trials. That when we choose to follow Christ, some things will actually get worse or become more difficult. That the world is fallen—broken—and it will hate us as it hated Christ. That we have to take up our crosses and follow Him. Love as He loves. Be holy as He is holy. Forgive as He forgives. Endure as He endures.

If we really want it all—all that God has for us—we must search for the blessings in the blisterings as well as in the bliss.

The good news is that there are *always* blessings in the blisterings. We just need to look for them. When our eyes are open to seeing the beauty in our brokenness, blessings flow, even in the bloodiest of blisters. Because trials are trials with all their pain and ache, but hidden in the dark corner of every challenge is an intimate, intensely personal invitation for us to meet face-to-face, heart to heart, with our Comforter, our Head Lifter, our Healer, our Tear Catcher, our Provider, our Counselor, our Refuge, our Lord.

FINDING BLESSING IN AN UNEXPECTED BLISTERING

Sometimes we come face-to-face with bad and even tragic news that we never saw coming. Life can turn us upside down at a moment's notice, leaving us spinning and searching for answers.

Ever been there?

"We just picked up your son for drunk driving."

"I want a divorce."

"Your position has been terminated."

"Your electricity has been shut off until you make a payment on your bill."

"You haven't been accepted into our program."

"I'm sorry, there has been an accident …"

In 2013 our family received some unexpected blisterings …

"You have a polyp on your right vocal cord and a nodule on your left vocal cord. In addition to that, Mrs. Smith, your esophagus is yellow and inflamed because of acid reflux. I know you sing and speak professionally, so I'm placing you on mandatory vocal rest for four to six weeks. You cannot talk at all. You will also need to adjust your diet and take medication in order to calm the acid reflux. If your condition doesn't get better with rest, medication, and dietary changes, you may need to have vocal-cord surgery."

As I sat in the doctor's office, I felt numb. The very instrument I used to minister and worship with was compromised to the breaking point. I wondered why God would allow me to experience a condition that threatened my ability to do the work He had called me to do. My feelings were a bit hurt. I pouted a minute in prayer, and then I saw a blessing in this blistering: the trial had driven me to His presence.

Two weeks later, my husband was told, "The biopsy and ultrasounds of your mass indicate that you have papillary thyroid cancer, Mr. Smith. We will need to schedule surgery to have it removed. Then, if the final pathology reports are conclusive for cancer, you will need to have a radioactive iodine treatment to ensure that all of the remaining cancerous cells are destroyed."

Really, God? Geeeez! Can we not have a breakdown here?

A part of me wanted to throw a toddler tantrum and give God a good talking-to about all the reasons Brad and I should be exempt from these inconvenient health challenges. Then, in His grace, as I prayed, wrote in my journal, and meditated on His Word, the Lord began to change my heart to see that good could come from the bad and that He would grow my faith if I would trust Him in the trial.

Through the cancer and vocal-cord trials, the Lord taught Brad and me lesson after lesson about how trials can grow our faith. These truths surfaced:

- **We get to choose how we'll respond to trials.**
  Trials happen to everyone. Doesn't matter who you are, what you believe, how big your wallet is, how thin your hips are, or how dark or light your skin tone is. Trials are no respecter of persons. If you're

breathing, you will have trials. The game changer? How you react to them.

One of my favorite verses is Proverbs 31:25: "She is clothed with strength and dignity; she can laugh at the days to come." Notice that it doesn't say she is kept from difficult trials. And it doesn't say that she is the source of her own strength and dignity. It says that she is clothed in it. She puts it on just like you and I put on jeans and a T-shirt. When we call out to Jesus for help, we're putting on the power of God to have strength and dignity in our troubles.

Every challenge leaves us with an option of response. We aren't destined for weakness or immaturity; we're destined for strength and depth in Christ. But you and I have a choice: Will we trust in God's strength, which is speak-the-universe-into-existence mighty, or in our own efforts, which pack no more power than the punch of a tiny flea?

Will we shake and flail in unbelief, or will we allow God to meet us in the wrenching and grow our faith? Will we waver in worry, or will we believe that God is with us when we step into the unknown? Will we acquiesce to the relentless waves of fear that come fast and furious or trust that Jesus can keep our eyes above the waves and teach us valuable lessons through the trials, even when the water is deep and choppy and scary?

Our trials reminded Brad and me just how important it is to choose godly responses, which of course can only come when our hearts are yielded to His leading. God grows our faith as we yield our hearts to His.

• **Trials help us prioritize what really matters.** Brad's and my health challenges brought the most important relationships to the forefront of our lives. We gave grace and apologized more quickly, spoke love more often, served one another without complaining, and were in constant fellowship with the Lord in prayer and His Word. God grows our faith as we unclutter our hearts before Him and ask Him to help us love others well.

• **Trials are opportunities for God to showcase His strength in our weaknesses.** Our sufferings can be redeemed and used for God's good. Brad and I had God appointment after God appointment because of our health crises. God gave us many chances to speak of the peace, comfort, and joy He was providing in the midst of our challenges. Brad said it this way: "He [God] moved my heart to look for what good He was doing versus focusing on my hardship." God grows our faith as we join Him in the work He's doing all around us.

- **Trial blows are softened with thanksgiving.**
Brad and I began to focus on what we had instead
of what we didn't have—and we thanked God for
those things. The Bible tells us that we're to give
thanks in everything (1 Thess. 5:18). In doing so,
the weight of our burdens was lightened. Yes. Brad
still had cancer. I still had severely damaged vocal
cords. The struggles were still very real, but our
pain was anesthetized with gratitude. God grows
our faith when we give Him thanks.

Now, on the other side of the cancer and
vocal-cord damage, we're grateful for those blessings that came in the blisterings. For the intimate
invitation God gave us to walk closely with Him,
to be held by His peace, and to depend earnestly
on His strength and provision. We are thankful.
Truly. We've found that in our thanksgivings,
there comes a release, because somehow in God's
glorious and mysterious way, He uses gratitude to
connect our hearts to His hope.

SOAK YOURSELF IN SCRIPTURES THAT BUILD YOUR FAITH

When you find yourself with challenges you weren't expecting,
soak yourself in scriptures that build your faith so that you can
experience all that God has for you, even in the midst of a trial.
Here are a few scriptural truths that strengthen my faith:

1. *God guards you with peace*—"Do not be anxious about anything, but in every situation, by prayer and petition, with thanksgiving, present your requests to God. And the peace of God, which transcends all understanding, will guard your hearts and your minds in Christ Jesus" (Phil. 4:6–7).

When I'm in the middle of a trial, I need God's peace to guard my heart and mind. This scripture shows me that the peace I am desperate for promises to protect my heart and mind when I do these three things: pray, petition (ask God for His help), and give thanks.

It might not make sense that simple disciplines of faith can make such a difference, but that's where the "transcends all understanding" part comes in. God is bigger than my understanding. His ways are higher than my ways. His thoughts are higher than my thoughts (Isa. 55:8–9). If I do things His way, blessings—like peace—are poured out. God's peace is powerful. And in His peace, my faith grows because I feel safe and protected.

2. *God hears your cries*—"The righteous cry out, and the LORD hears them; he delivers them from all their troubles. The LORD is close to the brokenhearted and saves those who are crushed in spirit" (Ps. 34:17–18).

In his book *Growing Strong in the Seasons of Life*, Pastor Charles Swindoll wrote this:

> Did you know that God takes special notice of those tears of yours? Psalm 56:8 tells that He puts them in His bottle and enters them into the record He keeps on our lives.

> David said, "The Lord has heard the voice of my weeping."
>
> A teardrop on earth summons the King of Heaven. Rather than being ashamed or disappointed, the Lord takes note of our inner friction when hard times are oiled by tears. He turns these situations into moments of tenderness; He never forgets those crises in our lives where tears were shed.[2]

It comforts me to know that when my spirit is crushed, the pain doesn't go unnoticed by God. That the same God who held back the massive waters of the Red Sea to rescue two million Israelites from the hand of oppression holds the minuscule tears that I cry in a bottle, stores them in the archives of eternity, and takes note of my aches. This brings me great comfort. And in my comfort, my faith grows because I feel seen and loved.

3. *God is with you*—God told Joshua, "Have I not commanded you? Be strong and courageous. Do not be frightened, and do not be dismayed, for the LORD your God is with you wherever you go" (Josh. 1:9 ESV).

This promise is seen all throughout Scripture. God will never leave or forsake us. Never. We church girls know this. But we also need to understand that this does *not* mean that bad things won't happen to us or those we love. And it also doesn't mean that we'll never experience pain, disappointment, droughts, or devastation. It means that no matter what we face, we don't face it alone. God—Immanuel—is always with us, and He can be trusted, whether He chooses to deliver us *from* the trial, *through* the trial, or *in* the trial.

LET HIM HOLD YOU

Life isn't always pretty. At times it can be relentless. Our hope, however, is found in the provision and compassion of a God who loves us
like crazy and hovers closest in our most painful trials. The psalmist
encourages us to "cast your cares on the LORD and he will sustain
you; he will never let the righteous be shaken" (Ps. 55:22).

Even when we can't see, feel, or sense Him.

Even when the jagged quills of challenge drive deep into the
flesh of a hurting heart. Rest assured, when you call out to God from
a place of desperation, God hears each cry, buffers each blow, bends
low to wipe salty tears, and lifts fallen chins. He rushes unrestrained
to heal your broken places. Perhaps not always in the way you want
and often not in the ways you expect.

When you surrender your trials into His hands, God works
through the pain according to His perfect will in mysterious ways to
bring about good. *His* good. Oh that we would want all of His good
and trust Him completely! The prophet Isaiah knew the benefits of
trusting God: "You keep him in perfect peace whose mind is stayed
on you, because he trusts in you" (Isa. 26:3 ESV).

Yes, pain will sting you, bad things will happen, people will hurt
you, and your heart will sometimes be burdened with heavy loads.
But God offers to meet you in the messy, prickly thick of it and use
the challenges in your life to grow your faith. He is with you when
high waters rise and will protect you in the midst of fiery flames.

I hope you realize this.

I'm struck by this thought: If there were no minor chords in
music, the songs we listen to would be robbed of richness. And what

would the world be without the depth of a ballad or a sonata soaked in melancholy? Even Handel's glorious "Hallelujah Chorus" has minor chords dancing throughout the melody! And so it is with us. Our lives would be robbed of depth, maturity, and beauty if we were kept from every strain and painful happening.

Every struggle is a divine invitation to experience God's intervention, provision, and compassion. To grow and mature. In responding to these invitations, we come to trust Him more deeply and to know Him more fully. So we actually *can* count our trials as joy. As gifts. Because if we want it all—everything and anything God has for us— shouldn't our primary yearning be for more of Him?

Jesus said, "Come to me, all you who are weary and burdened, and I will give you rest. Take my yoke upon you and learn from me, for I am gentle and humble in heart, and you will find rest for your souls" (Matt. 11:28–29). How will you respond to His invitation? How will you hug your porcupines? Carefully? Joyfully?

The apostle Paul knew all about trials, and he gives us a beautiful example of perspective in his letter to the believers in Corinth. He wrote,

> [God] said to me, "My grace is sufficient for you, for my power is made perfect in weakness." Therefore I will boast all the more gladly about my weaknesses, so that Christ's power may rest on me. That is why, for Christ's sake, I delight in weaknesses, in insults, in hardships, in persecutions, in difficulties. For when I am weak, then I am strong. (2 Cor. 12:9–10)

I read these verses and am challenged beyond comfortable ... stretched beyond shallow. This trial-welcoming joy rubs raw, but God has demonstrated time and again that His strength trumps my weaknesses when I place them before Him, and ask, and *believe*.

As I consider this, my mind scrolls through a few fingerprints of His faithfulness. He protected me back in high school when I wrecked my parents' car. He was with us when my son fractured his skull and broke his jaw in three places. He was there during the seven-hour reconstructive surgery and the six-week wired-shut healing. He was our provision year after year through the strains of job loss, job changes, and cross-country moves.

God is faithful, faithful, faithful.

As you cry out to Jesus, *expect* to experience God's grace and peace even in the times you face challenges you weren't wanting or expecting. You can trust that when you are at your weakest, His strength will rise.

When we hold to these hope-filled promises, you and I can confidently say, "I want it all—everything God has for me." I want to dive deep with Jesus. I want to respond well to the trials and challenges that come my way, knowing that they can increase my faith. I want to mature in all of the pressures that cause me to lean into God's peace, all the pain that leads me to experience His comfort, and all of the loss that makes me more compassionate.

Yes. I want to grow in faith, and if one way to do that is to go through trials and challenges, then bring them on. I want it all.

FOR YOUR REFLECTION AND RESPONSE

- What porcupine are you struggling to hug?
- Why is it important for us to know what God thinks about trials?
- What past trials can you now see as gifts? What blessings have you gained from your blisterings?
- In this chapter we looked at Psalm 34:18: "The Lord is close to the brokenhearted and saves those who are crushed in spirit." When have you personally experienced His nearness like this? How did this impact your faith? (Tweet your answer to me @GwenSmithMusic #iwantitall or leave a comment on my Facebook wall.)

Chapter Five

A FAITH BEYOND FEELINGS, FAILURES, AND FEARS

Nothing on earth compares to the strength God is willing
to interject into lives caught in the act of believing.

Beth Moore, *Believing God*

You can do this.

You can believe beyond your doubts.

Your faith can be strong in spite of your conflicts and fears.

Sometimes we just need to be reminded. I know I do. Yesterday was a whopper. My emotions almost got the best of me. Here's the recap: I rose early, worked hard, and was intentional, and yet I still felt unproductive. On top of that, we got a heavy heap of unwanted news in the afternoon: my dad has an aggressive form of cancer.

I can't believe I just wrote that last sentence.

He has been through so much. To explain the details would take a whole book. All I can say is that when it comes to the distribution of health challenges, my dad has had an unequally large share.

We found out a week ago that his ear was riddled with the c stuff, and that he will lose it. But I thought it was just an ear. I thought Dad's biggest challenge following surgery would be to figure out how to hold eyeglasses on his head.

The results of his full-body examination indicated otherwise.

The presence of disease is more invasive than what the doctors thought last week, so the ear, nose, and throat (ENT) specialist my parents met with yesterday removed himself from the case, explaining that the scope of Dad's surgical needs are beyond his abilities. Great. Today they meet with a specialist to see if surgery is even a possibility and to map out a treatment plan. Along with every diagnosis comes a barrage of emotions to sift through.

Far from my hometown of Pittsburgh, my Carolina family and I share the pain, fight back fear, and pray.

As I pray, God puts His hand on my shoulder and quiets my anxiousness.

Fears fade to faith in the presence of the Faithful One.

My heart still aches, but a peace holds me. His peace. Him. Jesus, my Prince of Peace. And as He holds me, I remember to exhale. To breathe deeply of His hope.

I remember that our days are known and numbered by a loving God who has a plan for each of us. I remember that I am not alone in this and that my Lord knows the agony of suffering. I remember that though this disease is completely rank, God is still good, and His strength is made perfect in my weakness. His grace is sufficient.

And no matter the outcome, life goes on because we know Life. The Source of life. The Way and the Truth and the Life.

No. This truth doesn't change the challenge.

It changes me and makes the little girl inside me feel brave.

It changes how I will face this challenge. Because if I'm really taking faith seriously, if I'm really telling the Lord that I want it all, then I have to trust Him to provide the courage I need when my knees knock and tremble.

We all have fears and anxieties to contend with. We worry about our children, our marriages, our singleness, our careers, our failures, our health, our educations, our inadequacies, our loved ones, and our appearances.

The truth is, you *can* stand strong when fear shakes you. (Yes, you.) Do you know that? Whether you're a college student swamped by studies and worried about that exam, a daughter struggling with the groans and unknowns of aging parents, or a stunned, anxious mom prepping to release your "I swear she just got her braces off!" graduate into the dorm rooms of a university, you can do this.

Seriously, you can. No matter what you face. This is important for us to realize, because the way you and I walk in faith tells the world about our God. It makes a statement. Tells a story.

We're going to talk more in the final section of the book about the impact our faith should have on others, but dip your toe in that thought for a moment right now. The world is watching. Do you want people to see your jeopardy or your Jesus? We all sift through feelings and fears. But when a Jesus follower is *consumed* by emotions and doubts, the world sees a weak God standing in the shadows.

Listen up, ladies: Our. God. Is. NOT. Weak.

And I for one refuse to allow my wishy-washy weariness to be the message that is showcased about the power, plans, and provision of God. Are you with me?

The psalmist said it beautifully: "You have been my hope, Sovereign LORD, my confidence since my youth" (Ps. 71:5). Like David, I've known the Lord since my youth, but I have to ask myself, *Can I honestly say He is always my confidence?*

Can you?

Becoming a woman of confident and courageous faith doesn't happen automatically. It doesn't happen just because you do a few Bible studies or teach Awana. And it doesn't happen just because you placed your faith in Christ. Courage *will* grow as you connect your challenges to the power and promises of God and yield to the work of His Spirit in and through you.

In the previous chapter, we talked about how the trials we face can help us grow and mature in faith. In this chapter, we're going to learn how you and I can stand firm when doubt and emotions try to shake our faith. How we can have a courageous faith that overrules the fears and feelings we face. Because if we want the courage God offers us, we have to expect that frightening situations will come and trust Him to provide the unshakable strength we need to face them.

I've decided to draw a line in the sand of my life. I am all in when it comes to faith in Jesus.

Yes. I can do this. I can do everything through Christ, who gives me strength (Phil. 4:13 NLT). It isn't just a familiar Bible verse that can be found on a T-shirt, bookmark, or bumper sticker. It's a truth I can cling to. A tested, timeless truth.

I know what you're thinking. I should wear a superhero cape with an adorable outfit and some really rad boots, right? Wrong. (Although I *do* love an adorable outfit and rad boots!) Even though *I know* that "with God all things are possible" (Matt. 19:26), I often still waver between doubting and believing. I doubt my abilities. I doubt God's. No cape. Just grace. Only grace. Because I'm learning that if I want all that God has for me, my feelings and fears simply cannot be the defining source of my faith. (But my oh my, how they try!)

FAITH OVER FEELINGS

The book of Esther shows us what our lives can look like when we trust in the sovereignty of God and expect Him to be powerful in the midst of desperate circumstances that could cause us to cower in fear. God positioned this young Hebrew girl to be queen of Persia so that she could rise up in His strength and courage when her people, the Jews, faced imminent death. She fasted and humbled herself before the Lord through prayer. And though it was risky to the point of death, she went to the king and courageously spoke up on behalf of the Jews. The result? God used Esther to save her people from genocide.

I want to be brave like that. I want to live with so much God courage that I don't go soft when life gets hard. So I take note of what Esther did. She didn't cave in to fear; instead, she fixed her focus on God and His power to save her and His people. She fasted and prayed and asked for Him to intervene.

Like Queen Esther, we can live with great expectations of God because He loves to do amazing things through average people— people with worries and warts and weaknesses, like you and me. If we want it all, we need to be women who stand firm when our emotions threaten to overwhelm us and courageously believe God for big things. We need to be women who *kneeel*. (Nope. Didn't spell that wrong! I live in the South. We often drawl out one-syllable words to make them two.)

I came up with this simple acronym to help us remember how to stand firm in faith when our knees knock:

K—Know Him

N—Notify my heart, my enemy, and my girlfriends

E—Express the mess

E—Exchange my will for God's will

E—Expand my heart in worship

L—Learn the Word

Are you ready to gain God confidence? Good. Let's get started. The first step we take is to *know Him*.

KNOW Him

Generally speaking, I don't trust someone I don't know. Plain and simple. I'm guessing you don't either.

God spoke to the prophet Jeremiah about the importance of our knowing Him:

> Thus says the LORD: "Let not the wise man boast in his wisdom, let not the mighty man boast in his might, let not the rich man boast in his riches, but let him who boasts boast in this, that he understands and *knows me*, that I am the LORD who practices steadfast love, justice, and righteousness

in the earth. For in these things I delight, declares the LORD." (Jer. 9:23–24 ESV)

The apostle Peter also wrote about the importance of knowing God. At the beginning of his second letter, he stated that the grace, peace, and power we need are connected to our knowledge of Christ:

> Grace and peace be yours in abundance *through the knowledge of God and of Jesus our Lord.* His divine power has given us everything we need for a godly life *through our knowledge of him* who called us by his own glory and goodness. (2 Pet. 1:2–3)

How can you know God? Read your Bible, study His character, and remember the ways He has delivered in the past. Such things are Faith 101. When you are overwhelmed by life, don't shy away from God. Don't isolate: investigate. Look to Him. Explore His goodness.

I learned recently about the familiar "trust God" verses in Proverbs 3. You know them. "Trust in the Lord with all your heart and do not lean on your own understanding. In all your ways acknowledge him, and he will make straight your paths" (vv. 5–6 ESV). The second part never made sense to me. I wondered, *Why would my acknowledging God motivate Him to make my paths straight? In the New Testament, even the demons acknowledged that Jesus was the Son of God, so why would my acknowledging Him make my paths straight?*

I looked up the root word and found a gold mine. The Hebrew word for "acknowledge" is *yada*,[1] the primitive root of which means "to know." It means "to understand, to grasp or ascertain; especially to be familiar or acquainted with." So, "in all of your ways acknowledge him" really means this: in all of your ways *yada'* Him; in all of your ways *know* Him and seek to understand Him; be familiar with Him; be acquainted with *Him*, and He will make your paths straight. Ah! Clarity! The key to a straight path, the key to trusting God when doubt shoves me off balance is way less about my circumstances and way more about my God.

When we're intimately familiar with God, when we don't just know *about* Him but really *know* Him, the most crooked roads we travel are made straight. Not because life is easy. Sifting through emotions like anger, depression, hopelessness, insecurity, and so on is hard stuff! But because when we *know* God, we know all of this as well:

> His STRENGTH that is accessible in our weakness
> His COMFORT that meets us as we mourn
> His MERCY that withholds the punishment our
>   depravity readily deserves
> His PEACE that defies our unrest
> His JOY that kisses the cheeks of our sorrow
> His COURAGE that makes our weary hearts brave
>   and casts away fears
> His REDEMPTION that reworks our brokenness
>   into beauty
> His LOVE that binds us to eternity and delights
>   over us with singing

Even when the one-two punches come and feelings are frazzled, I can confidently trust God by faith. Not because I understand all the circumstances, or even like them, but because I know Him. And because I know Him, I can trust that He will provide all I need to process pains, heal from wounds, and move forward in strength, grace, and peace.

That's step 1. The next step of the KNEEEL plan is this: when my knees knock, I need to *notify*.

NOTIFY My Heart, My Enemy, and My Girlfriends

I notify my heart of the truth of who God is; notify the Enemy, Satan, of the truth that he has no authority in my life; and notify my friends that I need their prayers (phone a friend).

Notifying my heart. A girl's gotta do what a girl's gotta do. For me, some self-talk often needs to be involved. Heart lies love to loom close. When they do, I talk truth to myself. (Do you know what I mean?) The psalmist did it time and again. Here's an example: "Bless the LORD, O my soul, and all that is within me, bless his holy name! Bless the LORD, O my soul, and forget not all his benefits" (Ps. 103:1–2 ESV). When I'm swept up in a tizzy, I remind myself of the truth about who God is: *Remember, Gwen. God has always been faithful to you. He has never left your side. He redeemed your life from the pit. He restores your soul when you park yourself in His presence.*

Notifying my enemy. Another important step is to notify God's enemy—and my enemy—that his plans to steal, kill, and destroy me aren't the plans of God. I take my cue from Jesus on this one and tell Satan that he needs to take a hike.

When tempted by Satan, Jesus answered with the Word: "It is written, 'You shall worship the Lord your God, and him only shall you serve'" (Luke 4:8 ESV). So when I'm confronted with emotions or failings that seek to gobble me up, I first need to recognize that Satan intends for these things to take me down. Then I let him know the Word, like this:

> *Satan, consider this your notification. It is written that I don't need to fear or be dismayed, because God is with me. He will strengthen me, help me, and hold me up with His righteous right hand (Isa. 41:10). It is written that when I pass through the rivers, they will not sweep over me, and when I walk through the fire, I will not be burned, because the Holy One of Israel is my Savior (43:2–3). It is written that no weapon formed against me will prosper, and I will refute every tongue that accuses me (54:17). So back off, liar. You have no authority here.*

Notifying my girlfriends. I'll keep this simple. We need each other. We're made for community and instructed to "bear one another's burdens" (Gal. 6:2 ESV). So when I find myself dabbling with doubt, I reach out to my besties and let them know I need their intercession. Here are a few Scripture verses that support this:

> Confess your sins to one another and pray for one another, that you may be healed. The prayer of a righteous person has great power as it is working. (James 5:16 ESV)

> [Pray] at all times in the Spirit, with all prayer and sup-
> plication. To that end keep alert with all perseverance,
> making supplication for all the saints. (Eph. 6:18 ESV)

> I appeal to you, brothers, by our Lord Jesus Christ and
> by the love of the Spirit, to strive together with me in
> your prayers to God on my behalf. (Rom. 15:30 ESV)

I want my sisters to strive together with me in prayer. To fight with me for the courage I need. And after I do my notifying, it's time to take the next step of KNEEEL: express.

EXPRESS the Mess

In this step I talk to God about how I really feel. It's important that I'm honest with Him. That I pour out my soul to Him. Hannah did. Remember? "Hannah replied, 'I am a woman who is deeply troubled.... I was pouring out my soul to the LORD'" (1 Sam. 1:15).

Hannah poured out her frustrations, disappointments, embarrassments, unmet longings, fears, and depression to God. I should too. Like Hannah, when I pour out my draining emotions to the Lord, He fills me with His peace. The apostle Paul encouraged believers to do this too: "Do not be anxious about anything, but in everything by prayer and supplication with thanksgiving let your requests be made known to God" (Phil. 4:6 ESV).

Once I've expressed my mess to God, I'm ready for the next step: the divine exchange.

EXCHANGE My Will for God's Will

Is it getting hot in here? This step leaves me sweating buckets because it is flat-out hard. Because I have a ton of ideas about how God should answer my prayers! *Sigh.* Instead, Scripture shows me that I have to trade in, throw down, and turn over my will to the will of the Father.

In the exchange I come to terms with the possibility that things aren't always going to go the way I think they should go. God is God. I need to give Him the space and place to be God in my life. Thankfully the Bible assures me that I can confidently ask Him for anything (Heb. 4:16), but I can't be so brazen as to think that the life-giving, all-powerful, all-knowing, perfectly righteous and just Creator of the universe is obligated to do things my way.

Jesus made this exchange of wills on the night He was betrayed in the garden of Gethsemane, just prior to His arrest and crucifixion: "Father, if you are willing, remove this cup from me. Nevertheless, not my will, but yours, be done" (Luke 22:42 ESV). If it was important for Jesus to set aside His will and submit to the will of the Father, then it's important for me too. So after this exchange is made, I continue to *kneeel* as I *expand* my heart in worship.

EXPAND My Heart

I expand my heart in worship by giving thanks. By moving beyond the emotions that try to consume me. By stepping out from the pain and putting on praise. It's comforting to refocus my heart on Jesus. To sidestep the struggle, I recoil from the flesh resistance of anger, anxiety, and doubt, and instead consider who God is, celebrate what

He has done in the past, reflect on the power He has to intervene, and respond to the love He has for me. When I expand my heart in worship, my confidence is augmented in light of God's glory.

The apostle Paul gave this heart-expanding instruction to the believers in the church of Thessalonica: "Rejoice always, pray without ceasing, give thanks in all circumstances; for this is the will of God in Christ Jesus for you" (1 Thess. 5:16–18 ESV). When I put this instruction into practice, the things of earth grow strangely dim. Which causes my confidence in God to rise.

Once I have knelt my way to worship, I take the final step of KNEEEL, which is to *learn, learn, learn.*

LEARN the Word

Knowledge is power. When I learn the truth, I earn the truth! How so? Well, when I earn something, I can spend it. Learning the Word is like chunking cash in the bank account of your soul. On a rainy day, you can make a withdrawal and have access to additional funds that can help you have strength when you feel weak, clarity when there is confusion, courage when doubts dwell deep, and harmony when things get hairy.

I love the way David shows us his unwavering confidence in God. This type of declaration is the perfect antidote for loneliness, anxiety, nervousness, and panic:

> The LORD is my light and my salvation;
>   whom shall I fear?
> The LORD is the stronghold of my life;
>   of whom shall I be afraid?

When evildoers assail me
>to eat up my flesh,
my adversaries and foes,
>it is they who stumble and fall.

Though an army encamp against me,
>my heart shall not fear;
though war arise against me,
>yet I will be confident.

One thing have I asked of the LORD,
>that will I seek after:
that I may dwell in the house of the LORD
>all the days of my life,
to gaze upon the beauty of the LORD
>and to inquire in his temple. (Ps. 27:1–4 ESV)

I've shared this KNEEEL acronym with you so that you can defend against the feelings, failures, and fears that come and go when life knocks you down. Apply the principles. Tweak it to work for you. Just remember: when your knees knock, *kneeel.*

YOU'RE BRAVER, SMARTER, AND STRONGER THAN YOU THINK

One of the most lovable and charming characters in the history of cartoon animation has to be Winnie the Pooh. He simply oozes adorableness and positivity.

In the movie *Pooh's Grand Adventure: The Search for Christopher Robin*, Pooh and Christopher Robin, who are the closest of friends, have a moving conversation high in a tree during which strength and love flow heart to heart:

> **Christopher Robin:** "Oh, Pooh. If ever there's a tomorrow when we're not together, there's something you must remember."

> **Pooh:** "And what might that be, Christopher Robin?"

> **Christopher Robin:** "You're braver than you believe, and stronger than you seem, and smarter than you think."

> **Pooh:** "Oh, that's easy. We're braver than a bee, and, uh, longer than a tree, and taller than a goose ... or, uh, was that a moose?"

> **Christopher Robin:** "No, silly old bear! You're braver than you believe, and stronger than you seem, and smarter than you think. But the most important thing is even if we ever part, I'll always be with you. I'll always be with you. I'll always be with you."[2]

This conversation always reminds me of the conversation Jesus had with His disciples after His resurrection. He gave them new marching orders and assured them that although He had to leave, they would never be alone:

> Therefore go and make disciples of all nations, baptizing them in the name of the Father and of the Son and of the Holy Spirit, and teaching them to obey everything I have commanded you. And surely I am with you always, to the very end of the age. (Matt. 28:19–20)

May these last words of Jesus serve as a reminder to you today that you are not alone or ill-equipped in your life. Because of this truth, you're enabled through Christ to be a woman of great courage and faith! Live like it. "You're braver than you believe, stronger than you seem, and smarter than you think" because the Spirit of God is at work within you to embolden, strengthen, and guide you.

Above all, remember this: God will be with you. Always.

FOR YOUR REFLECTION AND RESPONSE

- What emotions trip up your God confidence? Do you allow them to impact your courage and faith? Should you?

- Consider your current feelings, failures, and fears in light of the courage God gives you access to. Write a statement of trust on an index card or in your journal that boldly declares the ability of God to equip you in the thick of it. Keep it close. Read it often. Are you living with great expectations of what God can do in and through your life? Where would you fall on a sliding scale of 0–5 (0 = *God who?* 5 = *Expecting the mother lode!*)

- What do you need to trust God with today? What would trusting Him with that look like? (Tweet your answer to me @GwenSmithMusic using the hashtag #iwantitall or leave a comment on my Facebook wall.)

- Is your default response to lean on your own understanding or to trust God?

- In all of our ways, we're to *yada'* God. Know Him. Acknowledge Him. Trust Him. How can knowing God help you face your feelings, failures, and fears differently?

Part 2

———————————————

ALL THE POWER

Chapter Six

BRING. IT. ON!

*I want to live so that I am truly submitted to the Spirit's
leading on a daily basis. Christ said it is better for us that
the Spirit came, and I want to live like I know that is true. I
don't want to keep crawling when I have the ability to fly.*

Francis Chan, *Forgotten God*

Ever since I was young, I've loved connecting dots. In my childhood,
it was on pieces of paper with dots or numbers that linked together
to form an object. As I threw my attention to the page and followed
the numbered steps, a picture developed. A new creation appeared
that always made me a bit giddy. As if I had just solved one of the
world's great conundrums.

My grown-up dot-connecting challenges are far from a kid's fun
sheet. I continually struggle to make sense of situations and circumstances, and I long for a numbered life sheet to give me guidance and
direction.

If you have a pulse, I'm guessing you regularly deal with this dot-connecting life stuff too:

> *I'm confused, God. What is the right thing to do in*
>   *this situation?*
> *What can I do to help my child with his anxiety?*
> *How can I possibly forgive my husband for his*
>   *gambling addiction and lies?*
> *It hurts, Lord. I'm not sure I can go on like this. Would*
>   *You please help me?*

Do you ever wonder how to connect God's power to your daily choices, challenges, and behaviors? Do you struggle to understand how to connect the dots between your questions and God's answers? Between the decisions you need to make and God's wisdom?

The Lord knew we would struggle with this, and He gives each of us the power to connect our life dots.

How?

Through His Holy Spirit.

Jesus said, "No one can enter the kingdom of God unless they are born of water and the Spirit" (John 3:5). It isn't possible for you to become a Christ follower, to understand the Bible and other spiritual truths, to pray, to live set apart and holy, to be salt and light, or do anything for the Lord Jesus apart from the person of the Holy Spirit.

Welcome to the second phase of our "I want it all" journey! We've talked about ways to *live with* and *grow in* all the faith God has for us; now we turn our attention to the Holy Spirit, who helps us access divine power as He meets us in the thick of the daily grind.

In this chapter I'm going to present two key reasons why we need the Holy Spirit.

1. The Holy Spirit connects us to God's power.
2. The Holy Spirit helps us fight spiritual battles.

We'll also examine what it looks like to walk in the Spirit (versus walking in the flesh) and to bear good fruit.

Let me be clear about one thing before we go any further: this isn't going to be a Pentecostal discussion or a Baptist discussion. We aren't going to hang from the rafters, and nobody is getting dunked today. The Enemy we face is real—the Bible tells us so—and our lives give us all the evidence we need to believe it.

Here's the way I look at it: The Word is truth, and Jesus is the Word (John 1:14). Jesus is the truth and can speak only truth (14:6). If Jesus said that His followers would be better off without Him (16:7) and would do even greater things because of the One He would send in place of Him (14:12)—then who are we to pretend that the Holy Spirit is inconsequential?

Since Jesus made it clear that my life will be better with the Spirit of truth, I want all of the Holy Spirit. I want every vibrant connection possible between God and my life. I want every ounce of guidance, teaching, comfort, help, and reminder He will give me. Bring it on! This happens when—and only when—I live yielded to the Holy Spirit.

Excited? I am! Greater power awaits you, girlfriend.

Let's get this party started.

CONNECTING TO GOD'S POWER

In Scripture we see a beautiful promise. Before His crucifixion and resurrection, Jesus told His disciples that He must die to connect the sinful hearts of humans to the holy heart of God. He also explained that although He was leaving this world, His followers wouldn't be left alone or without power: "If you love me, keep my commands. And I will ask the Father, and he will give you another advocate to help you and be with you forever—the Spirit of truth" (John 14:15–17).

Jesus went on to say, "All this I have spoken while still with you. But the Advocate, the Holy Spirit, whom the Father will send in my name, will teach you all things and will remind you of everything I have said to you" (vv. 25–26).

The Holy Spirit connects us to God's power. He's the conduit between our problems and the solutions we're desperate for. Between our weaknesses and the strength we long for.

A few thoughts occur to me as I read these verses. Jesus calls the Holy Spirit "the Advocate." In the English Standard Version (ESV), Jesus called Him "the Helper." Both words refer to the Greek root word *paraklētos*,[1] which is a masculine noun that means He is our Intercessor (stands in the gap for us), our Comforter and Consoler (cares for our hurts), and our Advocate (pleads on our behalf, comes to our aid, and supports our cause).

If you're a good church girl, then you've seen all this before. You know who the Bible says the Holy Spirit is. But consider this question: Do you connect the power of who He is to your needs?

As I recognize my need for Holy Spirit power in my life, I begin to put the principles in action. Like this:

- When I feel overwhelmed, I can call on the Holy Spirit as my Intercessor to connect my anxiousness to the peace of God and to be a liaison between the needs of my heart and the Father.
- When I feel sad, lonely, or depressed, I can call on the Holy Spirit to be my Comforter to console my unease, lift my fallen heart, give beauty, and take my ashes.
- When the accuser, the liar, attacks me, I can call on the Holy Spirit to be my advocate, to defend me with the truth and argue my case before the Father.

Can you see yourself in any of this? Can you sense that the Holy Spirit can and should make a difference in how you approach your days and dilemmas? I can. Just writing about who He is helps me gain a more vivid understanding of the power I have access to.

Two other takeaways from that conversation Jesus had with His disciples gave me clarity as well. Jesus said that the Holy Spirit would *teach us* and *remind us* of the things He had spoken (v. 26). The word *teach* implies that there are things I don't know, and the word *remind* implies that the Holy Spirit will help me remember truths I do know but may have forgotten. When I ask the Holy Spirit to teach and remind me of the words of Jesus that I need to know, it's a whole new ball game. His power turns on in me, and let me tell you, I am desperate for that power, because faith is such a battle.

FAITH IS A BATTLE

When I was a little girl, one of the highlights of every summer was going to our family reunion at White Oak Park. I loved those reunions because there was always a seven-layer salad, yummy homemade favorites, and lots of desserts. All of us kids played fun games that filled us with laughter and drenched us in sweat. Then after the kid games were done, some adults would join us for a final competition: the tug-of-war.

When it came to tug-of-war, I had a strategy: wherever my dad went, I went. Because in my little-girl mind, he was superhuman strong. (I was ever the rational one.) Dad always positioned himself at the far end of the rope as our anchor, and his strength usually helped our team gain traction and, ultimately, win the game. (My opinion.)

Every day you and I live out a faith adventure that takes us to a different type of tug-of-war: a battle we fight against the invisible. Let's break down the competitors:

> **Team Defeat:** On the Enemy's side of the battle rope, the opponents are lined up and ready to *take us down*. They want to shove us into a dark, stinky pit. These opponents aren't visible, but they are very real. We know them: fear, doubt, guilt, insecurity, pride, comparison, inadequacy, indifference, and lies. Power zappers, all of them!

> **Team Victory:** On the faith side of the battle rope, the Holy Spirit is right beside us. He is

the anchor that helps us gain traction. He leads with the help that enables us to stand firm and be ready to fight. He teaches us how to be confident, compassionate, forgiving, humble, wise, and content. He reminds us of who we are in Christ and defends us against the thugs on the other side of the rope.

Each morning when I wake up, a tug-of-war begins again. Every. Single. Day.

I wish I could write from a place of perfection, but I can't. I don't always pick up the rope of Team Victory. The battle between walking in the flesh and walking by faith is as fresh as my morning mug of dark roast. And the pathetic thing is I *know* what I need to do even when I don't choose it. I know that I need the Spirit of God to fill and fuel my day with fresh power, which comes as He leads me in the perspective, peace, conviction, and truth of Jesus.

I need the Spirit of God because the battles are fierce. Are you whispering "Amen"? We simply cannot go into a gunfight with plastic knives in our hands. If I want to live with all the power that the Lord has for me, then I have to invite the Holy Spirit to lead. Every. Single. Day. The following pages will give some practical help on how to do this.

Let's break it down. We Jesus lovers need to be fully engaged and alert. You don't have to wear camo, but you need a battle plan. It begins with acknowledging that there is, in fact, a spiritual battle raging all around you, and it requires you to keep watch.

ACKNOWLEDGING THE BATTLE AND KEEPING WATCH

I was excited one evening because I actually had a fun dinner plan, which isn't always the case. Some grilled chicken was left over from the night before, so I decided to bust out my griddle and whip up some yummy grilled-chicken quesadillas. I know: it's a crazy-easy make, but for some reason, my kids think I'm a genius when quesadillas are on the menu. Go figure.

I grabbed a knife, a chopping board, and the leftover chicken from the fridge. Minutes later, the chicken was ready for its cheese and tortilla companions. While the griddle was heating up, I turned my attention to a few other family matters. I don't even remember what those matters were—just normal, ordinary stuff.

When I turned back to the business of quesadilla making, an empty cutting board glared at me. I raised an eyebrow and asked my husband if he had moved my chicken.

"No, honey. I haven't touched your chicken," he replied with a twinkle in his eye.

Hmm. A chicken mystery. How odd.

I began to interview each of my children, "Did you take the chicken off the cutting board?"

"No, Mom. I didn't touch the chicken," they said one after another.

I wondered, *If I didn't move the chicken and my family didn't move the chicken, then where is my chicken?* I looked around the room once more just to be sure that I hadn't simply placed the chicken somewhere else.

Then I saw it … a look of guilt.

A look that screamed and pleaded, *Yes! I took your chicken, but please don't be angry with me. It smelled so good, and … and … I'm a big dog. I need my nourishment. Was it wrong? Okay. I know it was wrong. Please forgive me. I did it. I ate your chicken. I'm sorry. I'd like to go to my crate now …*

His hairy ears lowered as my eyes met his. My brows furrowed. "Rocky! *You* ate my chicken! Bad dog!" I lamented in frustration as I began to make a new chickenless dinner plan.

Rocky's just a dog. He's not out to get me, and he didn't mean to mess up our dinner plans, but he *did* prey on our family meal that night. He came and took what wasn't his because I had let down my guard. I wasn't watching over my chicken.

As believers in Jesus Christ, you and I must guard our hearts and watch over our homes. The Bible warns Christians to keep watch. Beyond things seen, there are spiritual battles taking place around us continually. Allow me to state this again: If you are a believer and follower of Jesus Christ, then you have an enemy, and his name is Satan. If you live to listen to the voice of Jesus, the Good Shepherd, then strap on your battle gear, girlfriend, because your enemy has a mission to destroy you.

Beware!

The Bible tells us time and again to be alert to the schemes of Satan. To keep watch. "Be alert and of sober mind. Your enemy the devil prowls around like a roaring lion looking for someone to devour. Resist him, standing firm in the faith" (1 Pet. 5:8–9).

Though we have an enemy who wants to mess with our emotions, our health, our marriages, our children, our relationships, our jobs, and our thoughts, we aren't without help or hope. We have both. Through the Holy Spirit, we have access to God's power and protection: "The Lord is faithful, and he will strengthen you and protect you from the evil one" (2 Thess. 3:3).

I was caught off guard the night our dog Rocky took the chicken off the counter, and there have been times I've been caught off guard in the midst of spiritual battles as well. As Christian women, let's remember to call on the Spirit of God to empower us to keep watch over our hearts, our minds, and our homes.

STANDING FIRM

In recognizing that the battle is real, I'm also motivated to prepare for the fight. The Bible maps out my rules of engagement and holds my trembling hands until they calm. I must keep in mind that the battle is ultimately not mine. It is God's. And when I suit up in His strength, He goes before me and fights on my behalf.

In his letter to the believers in Ephesus, the apostle Paul talked straight about the spiritual battle of faith. He exhorted them to:

> Be strong in the Lord and in the strength of his might. Put on the whole armor of God, that you may be able to stand against the schemes of the devil. For we do not wrestle against flesh and blood, but against the rulers, against the authorities, against the cosmic powers over this present darkness, against the spiritual forces of evil in the heavenly places. Therefore take up the whole armor of God, that you

may be able to withstand in the evil day, and having
done all, to stand firm. (Eph. 6:10–13 ESV)

What help do I have to stand firm against attacks from Satan
and his cronies?

> Truth: Protects me against damaging lies.
> Righteousness (by faith through grace in Christ):
> Annihilates my sin.
> Peace: Guards my heart and mind. Motivates me to
> share the hope of Jesus.
> Faith: Protects me from attacks and extinguishes
> the flaming darts of the Evil One.
> Salvation: In Christ alone. Conquers death. It is
> finished. Team Victory wins.
> The sword of the Spirit: The Word of God. Inherent.
> Flawless. Guides me in all truth.
> Pray in the Spirit: Connects me to God's power.

How do I invite the Holy Spirit to lead me each day? By putting
on the armor of God in prayer and stepping up in faith to stand firm
in His power. (Note to self: review that list when I feel exhausted,
intimidated, and battle worn.)

I want to connect another power dot here. When Jesus promised to send His disciples the Helper, He linked the Holy Spirit to
truth: "When he, the Spirit of truth, comes, he will guide you into
all truth" (John 16:13). Truth has to lead my battles. When I believe
lies, I choose to join Team Defeat. (No thank you.)

Jesus went on to pray for us, His followers, that the truth would protect us from Satan: "My prayer is not that you take them out of the world but that you protect them from the evil one. They are not of the world, even as I am not of it. Sanctify them by the truth; your word is truth" (17:15–17). God's Word is truth, and truth protects us. It sanctifies us. Helps us grow in holiness. Helps us recognize the difference between God's ways and the ways of the world.

The Holy Spirit leads me to a faith with greater power because the Spirit of God will always lead me in the ways of the Word. Toward knowing, obeying, loving, and trusting Jesus in everything. I want that. So I pray with the psalmist, "Guide me in your truth and teach me, for you are God my Savior, and my hope is in you all day long" (Ps. 25:5).

Yes. Faith is a tug-of-war, but I'm not without hope, help, or power. And neither are you. Be sure to decide which end of the rope you'd like to pick up: Team Defeat or Team Victory. Because it is a choice, you know. When we call upon the Holy Spirit, who is the anchor of all things truth, comfort, guidance, and power, He helps us gain traction in every battle of life.

We gain traction as we're equiped to walk in the Spirit (instead of the flesh) and bear good fruit.

FLESH VERSUS SPIRIT

The apostle Paul wrote a letter to the church at Galatia during his second missionary journey. He was frustrated that many believers were wavering in their faith. Not good.

In Galatians 5, he reminded the believers that Christ died so that they could be free. And he was careful to distinguish that their freedom was not *to* sin but *from* sin.

He went on to tell them of the spiritual battle that was taking place between their fleshly desires and their holy desires. Between walking by the Spirit and walking by the flesh.

> So I say, walk by the Spirit, and you will not gratify the desires of the flesh. For the flesh desires what is contrary to the Spirit, and the Spirit what is contrary to the flesh. They are in conflict with each other, so that you are not to do whatever you want. (vv. 16–18)

How can we be led by the Spirit and not by the flesh? Paul spelled it out in the next few verses by identifying what flesh-led living looks like. Here's his list:

Sexual immorality
Impurity
Debauchery
Idolatry and witchcraft
Hatred
Discord
Jealousy
Fits of rage
Selfish ambition
Dissensions
Factions and envy

Drunkenness

Orgies and the like

"And the like" means this list is not exhaustive, but it should help us get the gist. All of these are ungodly choices that oppose the will of God.

My church-girl temptation is to look at this list and see how I measure up. *Am I good enough, God?* (Someone hit a game-show buzzer!) *Not* what I should do. This list should serve as a resource to me and as a reminder that while "orgies" and "witchcraft" might not be my biggest struggles, "fits of rage" and "selfish ambition" sure can sneak into my moments.

I walk in the flesh when I blow a gasket with my people, in traffic, in that email, or at my job. I walk in the Spirit when I ask the Lord to take away my anger and frustrations, help me sift through ungodly emotions, provide the grace He promises, and help me respond to my people in a way that brings Him honor and glory.

I walk in the flesh when I think more about myself than others. When I want to be first, be the best, have the most, be the boss, tell everyone else how they should behave, or demand to sit in a prominent position. I walk in the Spirit when I humble myself before Jesus, when I look out for the interests of others and esteem them as better than myself (Phil. 2:3–4), and when I serve others and give my life away for the sake of Jesus (Matt. 20:26–27).

Ultimately, when I walk in the Spirit, my life will echo the characteristics of Jesus. I will bear the fruit of His Spirit and choose responses, thoughts, and attitudes that exemplify the power of God at work in and through me.

Ready for one more list? Here's the *Vogue* magazine cover of true beauty. The fruits of walking in the Spirit are:

Love
Joy
Peace
Patience
Kindness
Goodness
Faithfulness
Gentleness
Self-control

I want the beauty of God's Spirit to be visible in my life. Don't you?

Paul went on to sum up the fruit bearing this way: "Those who belong to Christ Jesus have crucified the flesh with its passions and desires. Since we live by the Spirit, let us keep in step with the Spirit" (Gal. 5:24–25). There it is plain as day, one of the greatest challenges to humankind: the call to live out the love and freedom of Christ by laying aside all desires, thoughts, decisions, and responses that are against God's will and, instead, putting on the humility of Jesus and yielding our hearts to His Spirit.

If I want all of the power God has for me, I need to rely on His Spirit and look to Him as my helper, comforter, advocate, and counselor who leads me in all truth. "May the God of hope fill you with all joy and peace as you trust in him, so that you may overflow with hope by the power of the Holy Spirit" (Rom. 15:13). I pray this for you. I pray this for me.

Because I *want* to trust God for all of the joy and peace He will give me.

I *want* to overflow with hope by the power of the Holy Spirit. Yes. Yes. Yes.

I want the Holy Spirit to consume my heart.

Completely.

Imagine what our lives, families, churches, and communities would look like if you and I invited the Spirit of God within us to connect our life dots and prepare us for spiritual battles each day. Surely the world would see a beautiful, vibrant, powerful faith picture.

FOR YOUR REFLECTION AND RESPONSE

- How alert and open are you to the influence of the Holy Spirit throughout an average day? (Pick one: eyes wide open, awake but not necessarily paying attention, groggy and foggy, out like a light.)
- What major players are on Team Defeat in your personal tug-of-war right now?
- On a scale from 0–5 (0 = *Holy Spirit who?* 5 = *His hope is my rope, baby!*), how confident are you that the Holy Spirit is holding the anchor position of your battle rope?
- In what area of your life do you feel the Enemy is attacking you?
- What is one thing you'll do or believe today to help you stand firm in the power of God? "Today I will …" (Tweet your answer to me @GwenSmithMusic using #iwantitall or leave a comment on my Facebook wall.)
- Pause to pray for specific people and relationships you feel need protection.

Chapter Seven

KEEP YOUR DIAMONDS; THIS GIRL WANTS MORE

Every man is a ... fool for at least five minutes every
day; wisdom consists of not exceeding the limit.

Elbert Hubbard

Years ago I thought if I owned some diamond-stud earrings, all the stars in the universe would dance in one accord, and my life would dazzle. That year for Christmas, my husband dutifully scraped dollars and cents together to sacrificially buy this momma a set of modest but sparkly studs.

And guess what?

The stars didn't dance, and my days were no more glamorous after having the earrings.

Today I hardly ever wear those earrings. I got a second set of holes pierced in each ear to showcase the diamonds, but my ears get angry every time I put them in. Now the shiny studs sit in a jewelry box. My conclusion? Those diamonds are *so* not this girl's best friend.

Epic jewelry fail.

Epic Gwen fail.

I thought a sparkly possession would be the have-all, end-all for me.

Unwise. My thinking was faulty.

I'm not saying that diamonds are bad. I'm not saying that we shouldn't wear them or want them. Not my point. What I am trying to say is this: I make bad choices when my decisions are based on what I think will make my life better, more important, more peaceful, more blessed, or more impressive.

Things like diamonds are nice, but they're just fading flowers that bring neither blessing nor God's best to my life. It was foolish of me to think they would. And my foolishness caught my poor husband in the cross fire. He sacrificially chunked down some family change to make the gift happen. (Hide me in a small hole.)

Do you ever make foolish decisions?

Have any of your bad decisions ever impacted other people?

Yeah. Me too.

THE LITTLE BLACK DRESS OF FAITH

I'm really trying to grow in the area of wisdom. God has been showing me that His wisdom and understanding are much more valuable than things I often think of as valuable. The Bible places wisdom in a category far above the importance of gems or jewels or marital status or granite countertops or a Lexus or any position at work or any dress size I could ever have or long for.

It is so valuable that we're supposed to keep our eyes on it at all times:

> My son, do not let wisdom and understanding out
> > of your sight,
> > > preserve sound judgment and discretion;
> they will be life for you,
> > an ornament to grace your neck.
> Then you will go on your way in safety,
> > and your foot will not stumble.
> When you lie down, you will not be afraid;
> > when you lie down, your sleep will be sweet.
> Have no fear of sudden disaster
> > or of the ruin that overtakes the wicked,
> for the LORD will be at your side
> > and will keep your foot from being snared.
> > > (Prov. 3:21–26)

These verses put it into perspective nicely as well:

> Blessed is the one who finds wisdom,
> > and the one who gets understanding,
> for the gain from her is better than gain from silver
> > and her profit better than gold.
> She is more precious than jewels,
> > and nothing you desire can compare with her.
> Long life is in her right hand;
> > in her left hand are riches and honor.

Her ways are ways of pleasantness,
      and all her paths are peace.
She is a tree of life to those who lay hold of her;
      those who hold her fast are called blessed.
            (vv. 13–18 ESV)

That is pretty valuable stuff, friend. There are lots of perks to this way of wisdom! Rich rewards. I want to be a woman of godly wisdom. I want that sacred value in my life, don't you? Think about it. God knows everything, so when I choose His wisdom, I rely on the pinnacle of greatness to help me do and say what is best for my life instead of relying on my own faulty ways. Besides that, the opposite of being wise is being foolish ... and who in the world wants to be that? Not. Me.

Been there. Done that. Burned the T-shirt.

All throughout the Bible, we see that wisdom is the real deal when it comes to spiritual must-haves. I like to think of it as the little black dress of faith. An essential must-have for every Christian woman to possess and wear. And surely one that we all look good in!

GOD'S WISDOM VERSUS WORLDLY WISDOM

But in today's world, it can be tricky to make wise decisions and choices. We're surrounded by foolish and conflicting messages. Messages that oppose the wisdom of God as revealed in Scripture. We get hit from all sides with opinions, posts, and tweets about what people have and want and do—and about what people think is right and wrong. They write it on signs and walk picket lines in an attempt to sway us in their direction. They Instagram it, pin it on Pinterest, send e-petitions to our in-boxes, and blog about it. And then there's the media that screams like a colicky baby, demanding that we take note of the angle that *they* are trying to sell as acceptable behavior.

One thing's for sure, there's a wide difference between the wisdom of God and the wisdom of the world. When I say *wide*, I mean Grand Canyon wide. I mean the distance-between-the-east-coast-of-America-and-the-west-coast-of-Europe wide! Here's what James had to say about godly wisdom:

> The wisdom from above is first of all pure. It is also peace loving, gentle at all times, and willing to yield to others. It is full of mercy and the fruit of good deeds. It shows no favoritism and is always sincere."
> (James 3:17 NLT)

Does that sound like the world to you? Pure? Peace loving? Gentle? Willing to yield? Full of mercy and good deeds? Fair and sincere? I think not.

Keeping these truths in mind helps me as a friend. When I'm tempted to vent my frustration about that other person, God's wisdom reminds me to be a woman of peace. It helps me as a Jesus follower. When I'm tempted to read a book or watch a movie that is fifty shades of compromise, God's wisdom reminds me that I'm to be a holy, pure vessel for Him.

Here's a refreshing truth: When the world shouts its ways that are contrary to the wisdom of God, I have a choice. I really do. I might not feel like it, but I do. I get to choose my response even when the pressures of political correctness and tolerance squeeze hard. Even in my workplace. Those pressures are indicators that I need to address the issue and not run from it or cave in to it. My behavior is my choice, no one else's. And I want my choices to align with the ageless wisdom of the all-knowing God.

So I choose to put on my little black dress of faith.

And some cute shoes, of course!

SEARCHING FOR GOLD

Wisdom isn't always going to smack us upside the head with obviousness. Often the gap is huge, but sometimes the line between godly wisdom and worldly wisdom is thin. So how can godly wisdom become our go-to outfit for any occasion? How can we gain wisdom?

According to Proverbs, wisdom is a treasure we must search for: "Look for it as for silver and search for it as for hidden treasure, then you will understand the fear of the LORD and find the knowledge of God" (2:4–5). And just as every good treasure hunt includes a map and an X that marks the spot, the Word of God shows every treasure-hungry heart where she can find the rich blessings of true wisdom.

Here are three of my go-to priciples for gaining wisdom:

1. Fear God.
2. Ask God.
3. Seek godly counsel.

Let's take a closer look at each of these.

1. Fear God

Proverbs 1:7 tells us, "The fear of the LORD is the beginning of knowledge, but fools despise wisdom and instruction." I don't know about you, but I don't like to be afraid. Case in point. I was a tween with pimples; long, lanky limbs; and an attitude the summer our family went to Ohio to visit friends of my parents who lived on a farm. I didn't much care if these people were nice. I didn't much care what we would eat for breakfast, lunch, or even dinner. It wasn't the beach, and I wasn't overly thrilled to be in Ohio for a vacation. (No offense, Ohio people.) But I had heard they had horses, and that calmed my grump a good bit because, truth be told, I was giddy to ride one.

I just knew I was born to ride! My cousin Beth had horses, but up to that point, she hadn't had the chance to teach me the ropes. Finally I would have my chance.

The sun danced with a summer breeze the morning we journeyed past the barn out into the pasture for our horse adventure. It was beautiful. A perfect day for an eager girl to do something new and exciting.

I got a quick bit of instructions, and then I mounted the saddled creature, grabbed the reins, and ventured out into the grassy fields. All by my big-tween-girl self.

Freedom met me in the tall grass as Butterscotch and I became fast friends.

We walked. We cantered. We even galloped! *I was so good at this!*

And then I turned him around, back toward his owner and the barn, and Butterscotch got his *run* on in a fierce way.

Scared. Me. To. Death.

I didn't know what to do. I screamed, dropped the reins, and held on to the horn of the saddle for dear life. The owner was waving her hands trying to tell me what to do, but she sounded like Charlie Brown's teacher, and the moment was blurry mayhem.

Then when I was sure we would crash into the barn, causing me to meet Jesus way too young, Butterscotch came to a halt.

And I went inside to change my pants. (Joking.)

I was so scared that I collapsed into an ugly cry. Couldn't even control my emotions. And on that day, one thing became crystal clear to me: I do *not* like to be afraid.

Seriously.

If I see a snake, a mouse, or a spider (generally anything with more or fewer legs than I have), chances are I'm going to run the other way screaming louder than a middle-school girl at a Taylor Swift concert. Why? Because those creatures freak me out. It's an unsettling kind of fear. And remember? I don't like to be afraid.

Yet the Bible says we are to fear the Lord.

Come again? How does this make sense?

I've come to understand that the fear of the Lord is a *good* kind of fear; it's a righteous fear. The best kind. When God says we are to fear Him, He's saying we are to be in awe of Him, to revere Him as the One who dwells in unapproachable light. To recognize Him as the eternal eminence who sits on the throne of grace and lovingly welcomes us to encounter Him intimately as we worship.

I fear God when I reflect on His greatness, when I whisper, "Good job on that flower, God!" when I trace the jawline of my sleeping, whiskered man-child and give thanks to the loving Creator who created him. I fear God by giving Him the honor, esteem, and adoration due Him. In good times and bad. I fear God by recognizing that He is God and I am not. I fear God by understanding that all of the power in heaven and on earth is His. And in doing so, I'm ushered into a fresh beginning. To the greatest resource of power. To a starting gate that opens wide to knowledge, wisdom, and instruction—all of which are worth far more than any understanding this world offers.

Straight up: The world is a faction of fools who laugh at godly wisdom. It whispers venom to our souls …

"You don't have to pay attention to God."

"Do things your way."

"More! You need more!"

"It's okay to watch that raunchy movie or read that trashy novel."

Blah. Blah. Blah …

No thank you, world. I've got a mad crush on my God, and I don't need your misguided direction. The fear of the Lord leads me to wisdom in a beautifully sacred way. And that's a fear worth running toward full force.

The second thing we need to do to gain wisdom is to ask God for it.

2. Ask God

Four years ago we installed a new bathroom sink in our downstairs powder room. While I love the way it looks, I haven't loved the way it works, because the water pressure has been a dreary drizzle.

I asked Brad if he could fix the water pressure a few times. Let me say this: My man is awesome at a million and one things. He's super smart and a great help around the house, but the man has almost no plumbing experience. Being the great guy he is, he dutifully checked what he knew to check on the faucet but had no success.

Then one day a plumber came to our house to install a new kitchen sink. While he worked, he and my husband chatted away. After he and the plumber had become new besties, Brad casually mentioned that we had an issue with the water pressure in our downstairs powder room.

Once the kitchen sink was installed, the plumber asked to see the bathroom sink. Within thirty seconds, he not only identified our four-year-old problem, but he fixed it!

In thirty seconds!

It was a simple filter problem. Our filter had been clogged. For four years.

He unscrewed the tip of our faucet and rinsed out the filter, and then put it back in place. Problem solved. The water flows perfectly now.

The sink is the same sink, and the faucet is the same faucet, but now they work great because we finally asked the right person about our problem! The plumber knew all about sinks, and he knew just what needed to be done.

Hello!

It really doesn't take a genius to figure out where I'm going with this, right? We need to take our problems and our questions to the One with the answers. We need to ask God first. He can give us the wisdom we need.

I mess up on this all the time! I look to other people for help with my problems instead of first asking God. Don't we all do this?

We go to our friends, we ask our husbands, and often we ask Google! All of which can be good and valid sources for knowledge and direction. It's easy, however, to go to the phone before we go to the throne, isn't it? We run to people who possess limited knowledge and subjective opinions. Don't get me wrong. People can be great resources for wisdom. They just cannot be our *first* resource.

If you and I are looking for answers, direction, or wisdom, we need to go to God first. He is the source of all wisdom, all knowledge, all understanding—all that we need. Imagine what our lives would look like if we always asked God for help first. We could avoid so many troubles and gain great vision, clarity, and direction. It's for a good reason that we're told to "pray continually" (1 Thess. 5:17).

I can almost hear you muttering, "Duh!" under your breath on this one. Yes. It's simple ... in concept. The implementation of this discipline, however, isn't always our default response. For example, a friend starts to talk to you about that person who has her panties all up in a wad. What's your default? Do you automatically ask God for wisdom, or do you join in on the ungodly chatter? You know this type of stuff happens all the time! It does in my life. I'm learning that my best response is the silent prayer, *Lord! I need Your wisdom here!* And I zip my lip until He leads my response.

Most of us who have been Christians for any length of time aren't just familiar with this verse; we know it by heart: "If any of you lacks wisdom, let him ask God, who gives generously to all without reproach, and it will be given him" (James 1:5 ESV). Did you see that? When we lack wisdom—which we all do at times—we simply need to ask God for it. And He's generous with it!

Note that this verse does *not* say that He will give you wisdom *if* you've spent at least twenty minutes a day reading your Bible for the past week ... or *if* you commit five hours a day to homeschooling your eleven kids ... or *if* you've prayed through your entire rosary. It says that you need to just *ask* for it. You don't need to earn it.

What a beautiful reminder that no matter what we're going through, no matter what we've done, as children of God we always have access to the promised power of wisdom. All we have to do is ask.

3. Seek Godly Counsel

We've established that God always needs to be our go-to guy when it comes to counsel. Our first call. But the Bible also gives us the directive to connect with other Christ followers for guidance: "The LORD gives wisdom; from his mouth come knowledge and understanding. He holds success in store for the upright, he is a shield to those whose walk is blameless" (Prov. 2:6–7). The third way we can put on our little black dress of faith and find wisdom is by seeking godly counsel.

When I make an effort to seek godly counsel, I benefit from the power of the Lord that is at work in the lives of those around me. I benefit from their mistakes and from their successes. And it frees me from the pressure of having to figure everything out on my own. It frees me to move forward beyond my own limited experiences, faith, and knowledge.

Struggling with a tough work situation? Tangled up in a messy marriage knot? Are you being held captive by fear, doubt, and insecurity? Get some godly counsel. Proverbs tells us, "Without counsel plans fail, but with many advisers they succeed" (15:22 ESV).

My husband is a wise man, and God has placed him as the head of our home, so I like to talk through difficult things with him. He gives me a perspective that's often quite different from mine. When I need to hash out confusion, I sometimes go to the small group of women I call my besties. They are godly. They love me. They like me. They laugh at and with me. They pray for me. They mentor me and provide counsel.

We're all in different seasons of life and have different needs for godly wisdom. *I* am a poppy, *you* are a rose, *she* is a daisy—*we* are a wildflower bouquet! If you're single, divorced, or widowed, you might be the head of your home. If so, you could connect with a pastor for godly counsel, or a trusted friend who follows hard after Jesus, or a godly family member or coworker. Another person I encourage you to reach out to is the women's ministry director of your church. Grab coffee or lunch with her. She will love you!

There are many ways you can gain wisdom and add greater power to your life. Add to this list as you discover what works for you. Are you a journal girl? Write about the areas in which you need God's wisdom. Write a prayer in your journal that spells them out in black and white. Pursue the treasure!

And here's a wonky twist: sometimes God answers our prayers for wisdom by sending us to talk with someone who doesn't even follow Him but has the knowledge we need. When our son Preston broke his jaw and needed reconstructive surgery, Brad and I got counsel from a highly trained oral and maxillofacial surgeon. We prayed for the Lord to lead each decision we made and to guide the hands and choices of the surgical team, but our medical counsel came straight from the medical expert. His faith had nothing to do with it. Though that medical advice may or may not have come from a follower of Christ, Brad and I prayed for the Lord to lead with His wisdom in, on, and through it all.

God's Word promises that He will walk you to the understanding you need. Just ask. I know you want His leading as much as I do.

So when life gets crazy confusing, remember that you can gain clarity and power when you fear God, ask Him for wisdom, and surround yourself with godly people of wise counsel. In doing so, you'll find yourself perfectly fitted with a little black dress of faith. (Dance party!)

If you and I really want it all, then we have to want every ounce of wisdom God will give us. Ultimately, the Bible tells us that the treasure of wisdom is hidden in Christ. The apostle Paul inspired the church of Colossae with these words:

> My goal is that they [believers] may be encouraged in heart and united in love, so that they may have the full riches of complete understanding, in order *that they may know the mystery of God, namely, Christ, in whom are hidden all the treasures of wisdom and knowledge.* (Col. 2:2–3)

The wisdom you long for is hidden in Jesus. He is your treasure. In searching for all of Jesus, you gain all the wisdom and knowledge of God.

Run after Him, friend. Make this wisdom chase—this Jesus chase—your very own. Because when you run hard after Jesus, you'll begin to experience all the power God has for you.

FOR YOUR REFLECTION AND RESPONSE

- Where is your little black dress of faith? Choose one:

    A. "I don't have one, but I'm asking God for one today!"

    B. "Stuck in the back of my heart closet. I really need to dig it out."

    C. "At the dry cleaners! Wore it last week but need to pick it up today!"

    D. "Wearing, it, baby! Dazzling with His amazingness! Party on!"

- On a scale of 0 to 5 (0 = never; 5 = always), how intense is your fear of the Lord? How often do you prioritize Him, honor Him, reflect on His attributes, revere Him, worship Him in spirit and in truth, fall before Him in awe of His God-ness?

- What number on the scale would you *like* to be able to choose as your response?

- What are you going to do about it?

- Whom can you tell for accountability?

Chapter Eight

STAY IN YOUR OWN YARD

Although our sins are forgiven and we now have the power
to overcome temptation, we will forever struggle with sin
because we still have what the Bible calls "the flesh."

Chip Ingram, *True Spirituality*

It was a windy winter day. Our three dogs needed to stretch their legs and get a bit of outside playtime, so I let them out to roam around our fenced-in backyard. An hour later, my husband asked me where the dogs were.

"Out back," I replied.

"Honey, the wind blew that gate wide open, and only Rocky is on the deck! How long ago did you let them out?" he asked.

"An hour ago!" I exclaimed as feelings of unease crept into my heart.

Grabbing our jackets and shoes, Brad and I bolted outside and began to scour the neighborhood looking for our two little runaway dogs.

"Roman! Steeler! Come!" We yelled endlessly into the biting wind.

After covering several blocks of our neighborhood without seeing any traces of our dogs, I ran home to get my car. While Brad continued to search on foot, I began to drive around and call out for Roman and Steeler from my car. My stomach was in knots, my heart was gripped with ache, and my mind swirled with longing and prayers for our very-much-loved pets to come home. *Please be safe, doggies! Please, Lord, help us find our dogs.*

We searched and searched. No dogs.

Our phone number is on their ID tags, I thought. *Maybe someone saw them wandering and took them home to call us.*

I drove home quickly to check our voice mail. No messages.

I stayed by the phone in case someone called. Brad continued to search, driving through our development and the surrounding neighborhoods. After a long while, he returned … without Roman and Steeler. We were crushed. Though we had been praying for the Lord to help us find our dogs the whole time, with heavy hearts we prayed some more.

And we waited.

More than three long hours after the dogs ran away, our phone rang. Hope sprang to my heart as I heard the question from the other end of the line: "Do you have two missing dogs?"

"Yes, ma'am! Their names are Roman and Steeler! We've looked everywhere for them! Are they with you?"

"Yes, they are. I saw them playing outside by the street and thought they must belong to somebody, so I called them over. They ran right to me, and I've got them in my house. They're both a good bit dirty and a little bit scared, and the small one is limping slightly, but they're safe," she said.

The skies parted, and angels appeared in the clouds singing "Hallelujah!" as I grabbed a pen to write down her address. *They were safe! Thank You, Lord!*

Roman and Steeler had wandered over a mile away from our home.

Over a mile!

We scooped them up from the kind woman's house as fast as we could and rejoiced in their homecoming. They needed to be cleaned, cared for, and held. And that's exactly what we did: cleaned them, cared for them, and held them. Oh how we held them! And as I spoke with gentle, reassuring words to my small, limping dog, it wasn't lost on me—the parallels between my dogs and me. Between them and all of us wanderers.

God has established boundaries in His Word. They are beautiful boundaries surrounding wide-open spaces of His blessing, purposed to bring Him glory, allowing us to thrive in life and keep us safe from harm. Yet we wander. Oh how we wander through so many different gates of temptation.

I wander from God's best all the time. I walk through temptation gates like procrastination, overeating, or saying things I shouldn't say. So many gates, so little self-control. What happens is that my own desires take center stage, and my desire to please God in those moments is shoved backstage.

At the beginning of the book, I talked about my longings for a great life—to be a *beautritionist,* to pursue God's best and experience a maxed-out life of blessing. By giving in to temptation, I turn from

His will, turn from His blessings, turn from His best and choose rebellion. Ick! I make my desires more important than God's desires. And let's be honest here: the Bible calls this sin. (Not so gentle, right?) It's not easy to swallow, but it's true. And I don't want my sinful ways to keep me from God's best. I want to grow in Christ, to grow in faith, to experience His power, and to be a woman of eternal impact. So I need to own my sin and intentionally and prayerfully excavate it from my heart. I want to be a woman who honors God in everything. So it's imperative that I take this topic of temptation seriously.

EVERYONE FACES TEMPTATIONS

Temptations aren't optional in life. Everybody faces them. And while being tempted isn't a sin, giving in to them is. We *can* defeat the temptations instead of allowing them to defeat us. Scripture assures us that God gives us the power to resist every temptation when we ask for His help. Knowing this can and should affect how we respond.

What is your open gate of temptation? Is it worry, fear, or doubt? Is it that flirty guy who needs to be off your radar and blocked from your Facebook page? Whether your temptation is overspending or sharing the news you heard secondhand about that woman … whether it comes in a liquid that delivers forty proof or a jealousy that ties you up in knots … whether it tastes like sugar or smells like lazy, temptations are your constant companions, and they cling like wrinkles to linen.

The Bible tells us that God never tempts us (James 1:13), and since we know that, we have to conclude that temptations come from

God's enemy, the Devil. He slithered to the side of Eve whispering lies in the garden long ago (Gen. 3:1–6), and he slithers up to you and me whispering lies just as readily today.

A study conducted by the Barna Group in 2011 examined the type of temptations Americans struggle with, classified according to gender.[1] The results indicated that the top temptations women face "often" or "sometimes" are as follows:

> Worrying or being anxious—68 percent
>
> Procrastinating or putting things off—61 percent
>
> Eating too much—58 percent
>
> Spending too much time on media—44 percent
>
> Being lazy or not working as hard as you should—40 percent
>
> Spending more money than you have or can afford—39 percent
>
> Gossiping or saying mean things about others—29 percent
>
> Being jealous or envious of others—28 percent

The study also asked participants if they tried to do anything specific to resist giving in to a temptation. Forty-one percent said yes, and 59 percent said no. *Ugh!* Almost 60 percent of us don't even *try* to resist temptation! (Not acceptable.) Are you looking in a mirror? I am. And I don't like the reflection I'm seeing in those statistics.

It's high time I get uncomfortable with my sin and call it what it is. High time I move beyond my excuses and toward a solution for my corrupt behaviors. High time I think more about holiness than about my desires. High time I get over my gut reactions and choose to respond with God reactions. We talked in chapter 6 about Spirit-led living versus flesh-led living. Well, hello, rubber! Meet your road. It's high time I got serious about resisting temptation.

Are you in? If so, roll up your sleeves, friend. This is going to be work.

Here are two biblical truths that will be woven into the next few pages as we take a look at Scripture and craft our plan to defeat the temptations that often defeat us:

1. When I give in to temptation, there are always consequences that cut deep.
2. Every temptation has a loophole and is resistible.

Let's look at each of these ...

When I Give In to Temptation, There Are Always Consequences That Cut Deep

Travel back in time with me to Israel when castles were grand and kings ruled the land. At the spry age of thirty, David was anointed king over the tribe of Judah (2 Sam. 5:4). God's favor was with him. He reigned seven years over Judah and then became king over all of Israel at the age of thirty-seven (v. 5).

As the years went on, God blessed David royally. David built up the kingdom and worked hard to serve and honor the Lord. He led God's people with the principles of the Lord, and they prospered under his leadership.

Then about six years into his reign, when he was roughly forty-three years old, David's life turned in a devastating direction when he was tempted on a rooftop and gave in to his desires.

The story is well known, so I won't bore you with the sordid details. (If you want a refresher, pause to read 2 Samuel 11:1–12:14.) Instead, I'm going to share a few observations and applications that rise from the text in hopes that you and I can learn from history:

> *Observation 1*: David *stayed* when he should have gone (11:1).
>
> *Application*: *Be where you should be.* Historians and Bible scholars agree that as king, David should have been with his troops in battle. Had he been on the battlefield, the temptation would've been avoided.
>
> *Observation 2*: David *saw* (v. 2).
>
> *Application*: *Look where you should look.* David turned his eyes *toward* temptation instead of *away*.
>
> *Observation 3*: David *sent* and *strayed* (vv. 3–4).
>
> *Application*: *Do what you should do.* Walk according to the Spirit, not the flesh. David sinned when he entertained temptation and gave in to his own desires. He sent for what wasn't his and strayed from God's will in his rebellion.

Observation 4: David *swindled* (vv. 5–15).

Application: *Be honest.* Manipulating circumstances isn't God's plan for His children. David went out of his way to deceive and manipulate. The result was disastrous.

Observation 5: David *slayed* and *shrouded* (vv. 15–17).

Application: *Own your sin quickly, confess it, and don't try to cover it up.* Denial just leads to greater destruction. David's sin became an avalanche of cause and effect. His attempts to control the situation and hide his sin eventually buried him in a landslide of death—Uriah's and David's baby boy.

Observation 6: David was *snared* and *seized* (12:1–11).

Application: *Expect your sins to find you out.* God is very good at unearthing lies and deceit. None of our secrets are hidden from El Roi, the God who sees. He sent His prophet Nathan to confront David and communicate the consequences.

Observation 7: David *sobbed* and *spoke* (2 Sam. 12:13; Ps. 51).

Application: *When confronted with sin, repent. No excuses!* When Nathan called David out on his sin, David immediately confessed. He didn't make excuses, he didn't justify his behavior, and he didn't blame someone else. He owned it and cried out to the Lord (2 Sam. 12:13, 16).

Observation 8: David *suffered* (vv. 15–23).

Application: *Expect consequences that cut deep.* David and Bathsheba watched in agony as their baby boy suffered and died. David's sin affected not just himself but many others. Bathsheba suffered because of his sin. Uriah suffered because of his sin. Joab suffered because of David's sin. The same is true for us: our sin affects others.

The act of giving in to temptation always leads to suffering, because these actions turn us away from the will of God. Sometimes our rebellion leads to monumental consequences like the death of Uriah—or the death of my baby in an abortion clinic. Other times it leads to minor consequences, like muffin tops, stress and unrest, missed deadlines, or broken relationships.

I know this topic is heavy. I do. But if we want our lives to be amped up with amazingness in Christ, we must deal with temptation in a way that brings honor to God. The good news is when we learn to respond to temptations positively, the Lord grows us in holiness, strengthens our wills, and allows us to experience His power at work in the deliverance He gives us through His Spirit.

Every Temptation Has a Loophole and Is Resistible

Simply put, the Bible tells us that God won't let us be tempted beyond what we can bear (1 Cor. 10:13). If this is true—and it is—then that means you and I aren't doomed to failure when it comes to temptation. No matter what those potato chips try to tell us! I have a choice with every temptation. I just need to decide what my choice will be. To succumb to my own desires (to sin) or to surrender to the will of God.

Succumb or surrender. Those are my choices. Easy. As. Pie. (Not.) Which means that these types of well-worn excuses and rationalizations no longer hold any water:

> *I couldn't help myself.*
> *He was actually interested in me and told me I was*
> *   beautiful.*
> *The Devil made me do it!*
> *But it was on sale.*
> *I was just so mad.*
> *Well, she started it!*

My executive pastor, Dan Burrell, summed it up well in an email:

> God doesn't invite us to sin, and Satan can't force
> us to sin. When we give in to temptation, we

take an opportunity to face a choice and choose wrongly. The Christian, however, has more than just free will to help us choose. We have the Spirit of God, who faithfully enables, informs, encourages, and invites us to choose wisely. God does not allow the Christian to get into the place where she has a test that she is not able to meet.

Yes. We have the Holy Spirit sealed within us, and He can empower us to connect our challenges to the strength of God 24-7.

I'm so glad. Aren't you?

I'm always going to face temptations. You will too. It's inevitable for each of us. But I still want to live out the promises of God each day, to sidestep temptation, and to walk in the power of the Holy Spirit. To do that, I came up with six tools that can help me tackle temptations when the gates blow open. I'm pretty sure they'll help you too.

1. *Identify my top temptations.* What temptations am I most vulnerable to? Knowledge is power. Just naming them and making a list helps me keep them on my radar.

2. *Surrender my temptations to God.* I take my list to Jesus. I acknowledge them, own them, confess any past failures, and recognize that this is a heart matter that can lead to a sin matter. I hash out any of my desires that are contrary to the Word of God.

3. *Pray specifically and continually about the identified temptations.* If I follow this principle and ask the Lord to keep me from the specific temptations that wink at me most, I'm strengthened in those moments of temptation.

4. *Memorize Scripture verses that speak to my biggest temptations.* I can be quick to snap a sassy answer, so I've committed Proverbs 31:26 to memory: "She opens her mouth with wisdom, and the teaching of kindness is on her tongue" (ESV). When I'm tempted to reply with a 'tude, I turn from the temptation, adjust my behavior to the Word, and choose to honor God by saying nothing or editing my comment.

5. *Remove myself from temptation triggers.* No rocket science here. If alcohol is my weakness, I can make a choice to not hang out with certain friends who drink a lot or with friends who pressure me to drink. I can also decide to stay away from places that serve alcohol. If sugar is my weakness, I can decide to not buy sweets for my pantry. If overspending is my weakness, I can choose to cut up my credit cards and pay cash instead.

6. *Find an accountability friend.* This is huge. Having someone help keep me in check makes a big difference. So I found a Christian friend I trust who

has the courage to challenge me. When I asked if
she was available and willing to be an accountability
partner, she agreed. I can be honest with her about
my greatest temptations, and I give her permission
to ask hard questions and speak hard truths.

When I use these tools, I'm better equipped to face the temptations that will be staring me down in the moments, days, weeks,
months, and years to come. If I want it all, I have to want all the
boundaries that protect me from the dangers of temptation. So
instead of trying to pretend that temptations don't faze me, I prepare
for them. This helps me walk in the power of the Spirit.

James 4:7–8 says, "Submit yourselves, then, to God. Resist the
devil, and he will flee from you. Come near to God and he will come
near to you." And that is right where I want to be. Near to God,
doing life step by step with Jesus.

Want to walk with us? Obviously we all have different strides. I
walk quickly. You might stroll. It's all good, as long as you and I lock
arms with Jesus … and let Him lead.

FOR YOUR REFLECTION AND RESPONSE

- What are your gates of temptation?
- What would God's best for you concerning these temptations look like?
- Do you trust that God's boundaries are for your good? Why or why not? (Tweet your answer to me @GwenSmithMusic using #iwantitall or leave a comment on my Facebook wall.)
- Journal a personal plan that implements the six tools for tackling temptations.

Chapter Nine

THE POWER OF REST

One reason we are so harried and hurried is that we make yesterday and tomorrow our business, when all that legitimately concerns us is today. If we really have too much to do, there are some items on the agenda which God did not put there. Let us submit the list to Him and ask Him to indicate which items we must delete. There is always time to do the will of God. If we are too busy to do that, we are too busy.

Elisabeth Elliot, *Secure in the Everlasting Arms*

A few years ago, I was invited to speak and sing in Tennessee at a women's event, and to my delight, my daughter was able to join me. Prior to the three-and-a-half-hour trip, I had given Kennedy permission to use my iPad to watch a movie. Once we hit the highway, she got cozy with her pillow, put on her headphones, and turned her attention to the rectangular screen in front of her. Random giggles floated in the air from the movie watcher as I drove and prayed through the talk I would give later that afternoon.

It was the first week of November, and in the Tar Heel State, that's prime time for fall tree color. Just off the northern parts of the Carolina highway, past the congestion of traffic and the hullabaloo of the suburbs, I was freshly smitten by the splendor of God in traces of crimson, gold, orange, and coffee-brown leaves that were fluttering in the breeze under brilliant blue skies. The trees continued to boast of more and more glory as we neared Virginia, and then the mountains joined in on the praise party.

Oh the mountains! Pastor and author Max Lucado observed,

> Nature is God's first missionary. Where there is no
> Bible, there are sparkling stars. Where there are
> not preachers, there are springtimes.... If a person
> has nothing but nature, then nature is enough to
> reveal something about God.[1]

I couldn't agree more.

My heart was captivated by the glory of it all, so I tapped Kennedy's shoulder, pointed out the window, and encouraged her to lift her eyes, look around, and soak in the wonder. "Don't miss the beautiful," I urged. "Don't miss the beautiful!"

She paused her movie, took in the majesty, and agreed that God was indeed showing off His creation. Minutes later she went back to watching her movie as I continued driving, undone by the beauty. Overwhelmed by the sacred sanctuary I'd stumbled upon, I stayed in the moment and celebrated our Creator as the psalmist did in Psalm 96:

Sing to the LORD a new song;

    sing to the LORD, all the earth.

Sing to the LORD, praise his name;

    proclaim his salvation day after day.

Declare his glory among the nations,

    his marvelous deeds among all peoples.

For great is the LORD and most worthy of praise;

    he is to be feared above all gods.

For all the gods of the nations are idols,

    but the LORD made the heavens.

Splendor and majesty are before him;

    strength and glory are in his sanctuary.

               (vv. 1–6)

Worship poured from my heart as I gave thanks for the beauty show. As praise and adoration continued to rise, a God thought settled on my heart.

Tell them, Gwen.

Tell them what, Lord? I wondered.

Tell the women what you told Kennedy. Tell them not to miss the beautiful.

Ah yes!

I would tell them, and I would reflect on that challenge for days to come. How often do I drive right through the busyness of my days and miss the beautiful? How many moments of glory do I not even see because my eyes are too exhausted and worn out from my crazy life pace? You see, I am the Energizer Bunny. She is me. I keep going and going and going … often to the point of weariness.

Don't miss the beautiful, Gwen.

Through His Word, God has been teaching me that my weary is not His will. It's not even close to His best for me. And I want God's best. I want it all. I don't want to live life as a worn-out woman. And I am so over knowing that I have a problem and doing nothing about it. Are you with me?

GOD'S BEST REQUIRES REST

If there's one thing that can take a woman down and immobilize God's power at work within her, it's exhaustion. Get up, get the kids to school, go to work, wash the dishes, put away laundry, buy the groceries, jump in the car-pool line, help with homework, eat a quick dinner, get to the evening obligation, look over your list for tomorrow, brush teeth, apply anti-aging cream, fall into bed tired of being tired … wash, rinse, repeat.

It's really difficult for women to experience the beauty and renewal of God's rest when we're bogged down with busy. It can feel as if everyone else around us is able to have a full and fabulous life while we're sucking wind to get our floors vacuumed and our bills paid. Life can be draining and unsatisfying when it feels as though we never slow down.

I've lived this. I know the failure I feel on nights when I lay my head on the pillow and whisper the prayer, *Lord, forgive me for not making time for You today. Tomorrow, Lord. Tomorrow!*

The Old Testament shows us that David lived in the messy middle of busy too. In Psalm 23, David said that the Lord *made* him take a break. Yes. He made him do it. Read if for yourself: "The LORD is my shepherd; I shall not want. He *maketh me* to lie down in green pastures: he leadeth me beside the still waters. He restoreth my soul: he leadeth me in the paths of righteousness for his name's sake" (vv. 1–3 KJV). I love the way Psalm 23:3 is paraphrased in *The Message*: "True to your word, you let me catch my breath and send me in the right direction."

Yes. Please.

This. This is the desire of my heart. That I can catch my breath and be sent in the right direction by a loving God who knows what's best for me. So I … you … we have to be intentional. Life comes at us fast. If we aren't careful, the dizzy pace at which we live can unwittingly become our weakness and demise. Weariness will keep us from experiencing all that God has for us.

I know you know this. I do too, and yet somehow it still trips us up.

So what's a girl to do? I promise that I'm writing not from happily-ever-after fairy-tale land but from the very real front lines. We have obligations. We have families, jobs, friends, communities, and churches that need us. And though this breath catching will look different for each of us in the many seasons of life, our people depend on us a ton. They should. God tells us to put our faith into action (James 2:14–26). And we must. We must mobilize the hope we have in Christ. Serve. Show love. Feed the hungry. Minister to the widows and orphans. Yes. We must be women of action. But we can't do these things if we're exhausted and bone weary.

What it all boils down to is this: God's *best* requires *rest*.

Do you know that?

Now, let me ask you a slightly different question:

Do you live that?

The psalmist wrote, "Truly my soul finds rest in God" (Ps. 62:1). The gap between knowing that I need His rest and responsively living it out can be huge. Truth be told, I live smack-dab in the messy middle of this tension, just like David.

You too?

Saint Augustine wrote in *Confessions*, "God, you have made us for yourself, and our hearts are restless till they find their rest in you."[2] When we rest in the presence of God, He restores our souls. Rest is the central ingredient in the restoration we all desperately need.

If we want it all—everything God has for us—then we must prioritize rest. We must:

Reflect

Engage

Surrender

Trust

Reflect

Rest begins with reflection. The psalmists and prophets were masterful reflectors:

I will remember the deeds of the LORD;

yes, I will remember your miracles of long ago.

I will consider all your works

and meditate on all your mighty deeds.

(Ps. 77:11–12)

I remember the days of long ago;

I meditate on all your works

and consider what your hands have done.

I spread out my hands to you;

I thirst for you like a parched land. (143:5–6)

Our *first* call to action must be to focus on the Lord Himself. This get-with-Jesus business is the key to experiencing the maximum abundance that God has in store for every believer.

To reflect on God, sit in silence and fix your heart on the Lord. Reflect on His attributes, His names, His greatness, on the ways He has brought you help in the past. I often write out my reflections and expressions of gratitude. It might look something like this:

Lord, as I sit before You and allow my soul to breathe, I am reminded that You are with me in everything I face. That these troubles I am up against are not a surprise to You. Thank You for Your constant presence and eternal knowledge. I am in awe of the ways You fill my heart with peace when I sit with You. Thank You for meeting me in the middle of my stress last week when I was running late to work. Thank You for gripping me

with Your grace when I overreacted with my son about
his driving. I am grateful that You are my refuge. That
in times of trouble I can call out to You and experience
the shelter of Your love.

Another great way to reflect on God is to meditate on His Word.
For example, a few weeks ago, I was meditating on Psalm 34:5 and
wrote this in my journal:

David wrote in Psalm 34:5 that those who look to Him (the Lord) are
radiant, and "their faces are never covered with shame." How incredible it
is to know that God perceives me as radiant, not because of what I do, but
because I look to Him. My depth of beauty is rooted in the One to whom
I gaze. Help me, Lord, to look to my Savior instead of to my stumblings.

As you think deeply about who God is and what He has done,
invite His Spirit to work within you so that as you reflect on Him,
you become a better reflection *of* Him.

Oh that we would be women of meaningful reflection!

Let this truth sink in deep: *when you reflect on God, you better*
reflect God.

Our reflection *of* Him begs for a response *to* Him. Reflection
leads us to the Lord and interlocks our hearts, motivations, ambitions, and wills to His. This is where our faith fits together with our
actions, where our lives go from being our own to being His. Where
our thoughts and our thanks become our prayers.

After reflecting, the next step to experiencing rest is to *engage*
with Jesus.

Engage

Jesus understands how exhausting life can be. That's why He says,

> Come to me, all you who are weary and burdened,
> and I will give you rest. Take my yoke upon you
> and learn from me, for I am gentle and humble
> in heart, and you will find rest for your souls.
> (Matt. 11:28–29)

I love the way Jesus knows us. He doesn't pretend that we're perfect people with perfect lives. He knows we get weary, He knows we have heavy heart matters, and He invites us to His rest. He invites us to let Him share our burdens. To be yoked with Him. When His strength is connected to—yoked to—our weakness, those weak places become stronger because we are enabled to draw from His strength.

I sensed Him lifting the heaviness of my burdens during my dad's recent cancer surgery. In circumstances that were grave and heart wrenching, I experienced the strength of Christ as I cried out to Him on behalf of my daddy. My heart was lifted as I asked the Lord to guide the hands of the surgeons, the support of the medical staff. As I poured out my heart and yielded to His sovereignty, Jesus met me with His rest.

The Lord wants us to apply the wisdom we talked about in chapter 7 so that we're less inclined to find ourselves burned out. He wants us to learn to see Him as the answer to our unrest.

Life isn't always gentle with us, but Jesus always is.

He cares about you. He loves you and is committed to humbly serving you through the intercession He does on your behalf to the Father. He prays for you! How amazing is that? When you see Jesus more clearly and are responsive to this invitation, you'll find the rest He promises. That doesn't mean your burdens will vanish into a random cornfield somewhere in Iowa; it means that you'll no longer have to bear them alone. No matter what your feelings tell you, no matter what the naysayers tell you, no matter what your hormones tell you, you are a child of the most high God, and you have full access to the rest He offers.

When I'm exhausted, I pause to reflect on and engage with Jesus. And then I have to lay down my stubbornness in surrender. (Yay!)

Surrender

The discipline of surrender isn't a natural one for me, nor is it natural for my youngest child, as the next few paragraphs will illustrate.

I had been out of town at an event. Gone just one night. While I was away, my then eight-year-old daughter, Kennedy, had spent the night at her girlfriend Catherine's house. I came home to a groundswell of enthusiasm.

"Mom! We have to go to Wal-Mart to buy sponge rollers! They are incredible! Last night, before we went to bed, Mrs. Robertson rolled our hair in sponge rollers, and when we woke up this morning, our hair was *curly*! Can you believe it? My hair was curly! We just have to get some!" my flaxen-haired buttercup exclaimed.

My daughter is many wonderful things, but patient is not one of them. So the very next day, we went to Wal-Mart and got us some.

Fast-forward to that evening. I gave her a few basic sponge-roller instructions: "After your shower, blow-dry your hair so it's *mostly dry*. Leave it just an itty bit damp, and then I'll come up to roll it. And in the morning, your hair will be bouncy and curly for school!"

"No, Mom! I know how to do it. I watched Mrs. Robertson last night. I don't need help."

Right.

"Kennedy, it's a bit tricky. There are a lot of important little details that I can teach you, but I really think it would be best if you let me roll your hair tonight so you can learn."

"I can do it, Mom! I want to do it myself," the girl insisted.

(Yep. She's mine.)

And she rolled her hair … exactly as you would expect an eight-year-old, sponge-roller novice to roll her hair. It was a whack job. I knew that the rising sun wouldn't shine light on her finest hair morning, but I also knew enough to bite my tongue for the sake of the lesson she would learn. With an ache in my momma heart, I tucked her in and prayed for the best.

While it was still dark, she shook me awake. *Big* alligator tears falling. "Mom! It didn't work! My hair is a mess! Half the rollers fell out onto my pillow … *sniff* … and I look horrible!"

More tears. Deep little-girl sorrow dripped everywhere.

"Honey, I'm so sorry. It's okay. Just go wash your hair again and wear it straight for school today. We can try again tonight, and I'll help you this time." I used my most consoling mom voice … and stuffed down the "I told you so" that wanted to slip out.

That night after her shower, Kennedy blew her hair to mostly dry and then handed me her sponge rollers. As we sat on the edge of her pink comforter, I taught her some sponge-roller basics. Section off your hair evenly. Begin at the crown of your head and roll down. Tuck the ends under so they don't go funky on you. Give each roller the same amount of tension and secure them close to your scalp so they stay on while you sleep. Once her hair was rolled, she dozed off with tender expectations of curly hair.

Morning brought the beauty she had hoped for! I snapped a photo as she ate her cereal, because it was a darling moment. A little girl and her bouncy, blonde curls and unstoppable smile. Good times.

I wrote in my journal about the sponge-roller ordeal once Kennedy and the boys had gone to school, and I was struck by how stubborn she had been that first night. She simply would not hand over the sponge rollers to me, even though I had a lifetime of experience with the squishy beauty tools. Once she surrendered them, however, lessons were learned, and she began to understand the proper way to accomplish her beauty goal.

As I wrote, the Lord whispered to my heart, *You know, darling, you do this all the time with Me.*

And I do.

I frequently and stubbornly insist on doing things on my own. Without help from God. Without help from the One who is all-wise, all-knowing, all-powerful, all-gracious, and fully able.

Perhaps you do too?

Oh that we would hand over our sponge rollers to the Master Beautician and allow Him to craft a work of radiance in and through us. I constantly pray as David did, "Teach me your way, LORD, that I may rely on your faithfulness; give me an undivided heart, that I may fear your name" (Ps. 86:11).

I surrender!

Your way, Lord.

Your way.

Not mine.

The last thing you and I want to do is be stubborn with God. I'm learning that the beauty of surrender is this: when I lay down my mess, my hands are then free to pick up God's rest. Keep that one tucked away in your heart as a prayer for the times you want to cling to your sponge rollers. *Lord, please help me lay down my mess and pick up Your rest!*

Our kinks begin to smooth out nicely as we reflect, engage, and surrender. The final step for us to experience God's rest is that we trust Him.

Trust

In times of trial, it can be hard for us to believe that God is working things out for good. In the first section of this book, we established that God can use all our trials to grow our faith and bring Him glory. Let's talk now about how we can have the powerful peace we long for by choosing to trust God. Peace that leads us beyond our what-ifs and whys … all the way to God's rest.

The apostle Paul instructed,

> Do not be anxious about anything, but in every-
> thing by prayer and supplication with thanksgiving
> let your requests be made known to God. And the
> peace of God, which surpasses all understanding,

will guard your hearts and your minds in Christ
Jesus. (Phil. 4:6–7 ESV)

Are you anxious about anything? Have you talked to God about
it? Have you given Him thanks? Have you laid it down? If so, then
don't pick it back up. Instead, choose to pick up God's rest.

Jesus said this to a crowd of average, ordinary listeners, people
just like you and me:

> Can any one of you by worrying add a single hour
> to your life? … So do not worry, saying, "What
> shall we eat?" or "What shall we drink?" or "What
> shall we wear?" For the pagans run after all these
> things, and your heavenly Father knows that you
> need them. (Matt. 6:27, 31–32)

Worrying might be your natural response, but it doesn't have to
be your *chosen* response. It doesn't add time to your life. It doesn't
bring rest to your life. Jesus said so, and He doesn't lie. God wants
you to trust Him.

Make that choice. Trust Him.

Friend, your heavenly Father knows that your job is stressing you
out, that your marriage is hanging by a thread, that you're bogged
down with health challenges, that you're grieving that loss, that your
finances are upside down. He knows the longings of your heart.

He. Knows. What. You. Need.

Knowing that *He* knows what we need should change the
way you and I trust Him. Think about it. What would happen if

every morning you woke up and decided to REST? What if you determined each day and in every weary moment to choose to trust God for what you need because you know that *He knows* what you need?

Can you imagine living with that kind of faith? With that kind of power?

That is exactly what the Lord is inviting you into.

His peace.

His rest.

His best.

Don't miss the beautiful, girlfriend. God invites us to be renewed and restored in His presence. In Him we find rest and gain strength. If we want it all—everything God has for us—then we must prioritize practicing the presence of God. We must REST.

When you reflect, engage, surrender, and trust, don't expect that your life will be perfect. It won't be. The promise is that you will be equipped for every trial, stress, and strain in the all-sufficient grace the Lord provides. Because the One who captures you in surrender is the One who sets you free in rest. In the surrender, God empowers you to trust Him more … and the beauty of the Master Beautician will be noticeable in your bounce and in your curls.

FOR YOUR REFLECTION AND RESPONSE

- Do you contend with any emotions or difficulties that consume your thoughts and block you from seeing the beauty that is all around you? What are they?
- What are your sponge rollers? (The things you don't want to release to God.)
- What would it look like if you accepted the charge to hand them over to God?
- Think of a time when you laid down your mess and picked up God's rest. How did that feel? Did anyone around you notice? Do you think God noticed? Why or why not?
- What is *one thing* you can do this week to position yourself more deeply in God's rest? (Tweet your answer to me @GwenSmithMusic using #iwantitall or leave a comment on my Facebook wall.)

Chapter Ten

WHETHER LIFE IS CALM OR COMPLICATED, DO THIS

Prayer is the exercise of drawing on the grace of God.

Oswald Chambers, *My Utmost for His Highest*

Pump up the volume

Pump up the volume

Pump up the volume

Dance! Dance![1]

My inner-eighties chick strikes again.

(You're welcome. I know it's in your head now.)

It's time to talk about prayer. I want all the power God has for me, and I'm convinced that there is a strong connection between the prayers I pray and the power I experience. I know what it's like to feel God's power. Totally love it. And I know what it's like to wonder if my life has been unplugged from it. Totally hate it.

By no means will I try to convince you that I've figured out all the ways to pray effectively. I have, however, found a few personal prayer points that "pump up the volume" of God's power in my life: grab the magnification mirror, extend God an all-out pass, and wait in expectation.

GRAB THE MAGNIFICATION MIRROR

A few years ago, my mother-in-law gave me a 12x magnification hand mirror as part of a gift. She told me that she uses hers all the time and expected that I would love it. Never thinking I would actually need or use it, I thanked her with all the grace I could muster and put the mirror away where I put the gifts I never plan on needing or using. (C'mon. I know you have a spot in your house for that kind of gift too!)

Fast-forward a few years … My teenage son was working on a self-portrait for art class and asked me if I had a hand mirror. I remembered that the 12x magnification mirror had a normal-mirror side, so I ran and got it for him.

After his art project was completed, Preston placed the mirror in the top drawer of my bathroom vanity. (*So* not where it had been!) Not long after that, on a grooming day, I reached for my tweezers to pluck what needed plucking, and in doing so, my eyes fell upon the 12x magnification mirror.

What the heck! I'll try it, I thought.

(Insert freaky horror sounds here …)

I wasn't at all prepared for the revelation of my up-close and personal reflection. My pores looked like swimming pools, and my stray eyebrow hairs looked like tree trunks. Even the supertiny, fine ones!

It. Was. Crazy.

And I must tell you, eyebrow plucking has never been the same for me since!

Here's why: prior to having this hypermagnified experience, I'd always thought I did a good job plucking my eyebrows. Wrong! Though I used to *think* I did a good job plucking, now I *know* that I do, because what isn't visible to me in a normal mirror is vibrantly visible in the magnified one. So now every stray that doesn't belong gets gone!

Over the years I've found that it's far too easy to pray in a way that's similar to how I used to pluck my eyebrows. I confessed only the sins that were visible in my life, leaving me blissfully unaware of the smaller, harder-to-see stray responses, attitudes, thought patterns, and wrong choices that needed to be plucked as well. Have you ever pretended that everything is just peachy with God when you knew it wasn't? It's easier. I know. Have you ever felt justified holding on to unforgiveness even though you knew God was requiring you to release it? Have you ever lived with a guy, or been sexually active with a man, who wasn't your husband and kept praying for your relationship to be blessed? Time to get real.

If you and I want all that God has for us, we gotta pluck those strays—any choices we make that go against the ways of God that are revealed in His Word. Disobedience diminishes the power He has for our lives.

We all have rebellion rushing through the veins of our hearts. For me it could be things like pride, arrogance, complacency, self-centeredness, and doubt—or being overly concerned about what *other people* are doing, buying, posting, wearing, and saying. For you it could be laziness or promiscuity or overspending or rage.

Any thought we think or choice we make that doesn't line up with the holy ways of God will keep us from the fullness of His power. The Holy Spirit is kind enough to tap us on our stubborn shoulders and suggest we bend a knee to hash it out and clear it up (Rom. 2:4).

Like David, we need to cry out, "Search me, God, and know my heart; test me and know my anxious thoughts. See if there is any offensive way in me, and lead me in the way everlasting" (Ps. 139: 23–24). That's a 12x-magnified prayer, my friend! David prayed for purposed purity to rise. We need to do the same.

If you and I can get this, if we'll stop playing good-girl Sunday school games, get real with God, and ask Him to reveal and remove the stray sins from our lives, the Spirit of God will lead us to new heights, widths, and depths of His love, purity, and power. This grooming will lead to your blooming! (Bloom on, flower!)

The next prayer point that brings blessing and power is this: when you pray, always invite God into your day.

EXTEND GOD AN ALL-ACCESS PASS

Norman Grubb was a humble British missionary in the early 1900s. He told the world that his life began to change when he started praying the same simple prayer each morning: "Good morning, Lord! What are You up to today? Can I be a part of it? Thank You. Amen." He invited himself into the story that God was writing in the lives of those around him.

I've been waking up with a similar prayer on my lips since the message of this book began to unravel my heart in beautiful ways:

Lord, I want it all today! Every blessing You ordain. Every trial, every strain. Break and build me for Your gain. Humbly now I ask You, lead. Give me Your strength where I am weak. Guide each choice and every gaze. Stir my soul to sing Your praise.

I ask for God's guidance every morning. I invite Him to bless my average with His amazing. I ask Him to teach me, use me, and show me what He's up to. And sometimes He surprises me in extra-special ways that blow me away. Like this …

It's completely normal for me to run late. Especially when I'm trying to catch a flight. On this particular day, however, I arrived at the airport much earlier than normal. I was faced with a dilemma: pay seventy-five dollars and get home two hours earlier, or save the money and enjoy some time to relax and reflect on the conference I had just left. Not feeling that I could justify the added expense, I checked my luggage, went through security, and boarded the train that would take me to my gate in terminal B.

With time to kill and a tummy to fill, I eyed the TGI Fridays located near my gate, B21, and then walked into the restaurant. The hostess led me toward the back room to be seated.

"Can I sit here instead?" I asked as we passed by a tiny booth in the middle of the restaurant.

"Sure!" she replied. "Your server will be with you in a moment."

A beautiful young woman I'll call Bria greeted me. She liked my hair. I liked her friendliness. She told me about her two littles, a boy and a girl who were two and three. I told her about my teenagers who were growing up way too fast. We shared smiles and conversation; then she took my drink order, and I turned my attention to the menu.

After she came back with my drink and recommended the salmon, I told her that I would be praying for my meal and asked her if there was anything I could pray for her about.

"Yes!" she said, seeming somewhat amazed that I had asked. "That would be great. My husband has a court date this week, and we really need prayer."

Tears puddled in her eyes.

As she continued to wait on tables, I prayed.

When Bria came back to my table, she asked me what I do for a living. I told her.

"What is your husband going to court for?" I asked.

Serious face. "He was just doing a favor for a friend. The lawyers can't even believe he was charged.... It's a really bad situation ... prison bad."

"If convicted, how long could he possibly be in prison?" I asked gently.

"Ten to twenty years," she said with eyes that searched mine for hope. "I'm really scared."

"Oh, man. I'm sorry. That's hard stuff."

She waited on a few more customers. I prayed.

When she brought my check, she looked me in the eye, leaned in close, and softly said, "This morning I prayed and asked God to send me a sign." Then she leaned in a little closer and said, "I believe you are my sign. Thank you *so* much."

Wow. Chill bumps.

I agreed and told her that the Lord surely wants her to know that she is loved and that He is listening. We said good-bye as new friends, knowing that we had both just experienced God.

I paid my bill and headed to my gate: B21.

I was early for my flight, so I wasn't surprised to see that the gate's notification board didn't say that the next flight was to Charlotte, North Carolina. After a few minutes, I looked up and realized that the flight on the board was too close to my flight time to make sense. So I pulled out my ticket and looked at my gate number.

My ticket said D21! That was in a completely different terminal.

No. Way.

And right away *I knew*.

I knew that the Lord had me arrive at the airport early. I knew that He led me to pass up the earlier flight. I knew that He had placed B21 in my mind so that I would go to terminal B and connect with Bria.

Before heading to the train that would take me to the D terminal, I ran back into the restaurant to find her.

"Bria! Just wanted to let you know that my gate is D21. For some reason I thought I was flying out of B21. You're the reason. God really *did* send me to be your sign. He's listening."

Oh the look she gave me.

My chill bumps had chill bumps.

Does God really hear our prayers? You bet He does.

Does God want us to extend Him an all-access pass to our days? Oh yes.

The grace of Jesus held us close as Bria and I hugged and said another quick good-bye. Then I headed to terminal D with a fresh awe for a God who loves so much and listens so attentively. "I will honor and praise your name, for you are my God. You do such wonderful things! You planned them long ago, and now you have accomplished them" (Isa. 25:1 NLT).

When we extend God an invitation to use us, He shows up in powerful ways. Add this step of invitation to your times of prayer. Open your heart to the ways God is at work in the lives of others and be ready to enter their God stories. God is all about exciting faith adventures! The final prayer point that helps me is this: wait in expectation.

WAIT IN EXPECTATION

The Bible tells us that "faith is the assurance of things hoped for, the conviction of things not seen" (Heb. 11:1 ESV). The writer of Hebrews goes on to tell us that without faith it is impossible to please God. *Impossible.* Take that in. It also says that those of us who draw near to God need to "believe that he exists and that he rewards those who seek him" (v. 6 ESV).

I wonder … does my faith please God? Do I believe Him a lot or just a little? At times I find myself on autopilot when I pray. Especially when the sun is shining and the world is right. I forget the active nature of believing and fall into passivity. Believing is a choice that must be made with every prayer, not just one time. In the passivity, I forget to expect big things from Him. Or I stomp my feet and demand that He answer me now, *now*, NOW!

Do you ever do that? Do you ever pray—because it's what we Jesus girls do—but forget to think big thoughts about God and expect great things from Him? Do you ever get bossy with your prayers and try to tell God how you think He should take care of your situation? (Hang on. I just stubbed my toe on that one.) Do you ever pray for big things but doubt that God even hears you? Do you ever doubt His power? Don't fret. Doubts are going to happen. Paul Tournier said, "Where there is no longer any opportunity for doubt, there is no longer any opportunity for faith either."[2] Jesus said that everything is possible for one who believes (Mark 9:23). When in doubt, I often throw up a simple prayer like the man in Mark 9:24: *I believe; help my unbelief!*

I'm convinced that our lack of belief diminishes the power God wants to amplify through our great expectations of Him. The good news is that He meets honest hearts in the middle of unbelief and helps us wait in expectation.

I want every ounce of power God has for me, but I'm going to be honest with you: there are times when I feel as though I'm in a trash compactor with the walls closing in. Times when I pray and fight tooth and nail to experience that *all-is-well* peace.

I'm actually there now.

Today I am praying for my son, who just had surgery and is facing a four-month recovery. I'm praying for a forty-two-year-old friend who was diagnosed a year ago with breast cancer, had a double mastectomy, chemo, radiation, and reconstruction. She was on the road to healing. Doing great. Only to find out last week that she now has stage-four cancer in her spine. She is the matriarch to a household of boys. She is a rose among thorns. Thorns need their rose. She's been given one to three years to live.

I'm also praying for Jennifer, one of my best friends from college. She was in my wedding. I was in hers. Anne of Green Gables would call her a bosom friend, a kindred spirit. The kind you can catch up with every few years and feel as if you never missed a beat. Her husband, Joe, had surgery for a rare stomach cancer a couple of weeks ago. Joe was making good progress. Walking the halls. Setting daily health goals with his nurses each morning. Then on Saturday morning, he took a turn for the worse and died. Shocking everybody. Leaving my college bestie a widow and their two children fatherless. (I hate, hate, hate cancer!)

And there are other loved ones struggling too. So many others. I know your list is just as long as mine.

I pray … and at times I feel like curling up in a fetal position.

The walls are pressing hard. The aches are real. The groanings are raw.

Under the weight of it all, I'm thankful for what I know of God. For what I know of His power. I know that God is in the middle of it all. That He is right beside me. Right beside them. I know that He is more than able to handle complicated challenges and is faithful to provide the grace needed for each broken moment.

I also know that without His strength I crumble. Without His presence I panic. Without His Spirit I wander and wonder and wane. When David was in duress, he often spoke to himself in the Psalms. I love that … because I do it too sometimes. "Find rest, O my soul, in God alone; my hope comes from him" (Ps. 62:5 NIV 1984).

I turn my heart toward God and talk to myself. *Keep calm, Gwen. God is still on the throne, and you are free to approach Him at any time, with any ache, with any question, with any weakness. Thank You, Jesus.*

I love the way *The Message* paraphrases the encouraging verses of Ephesians 3:20: "God can do anything, you know—far more than you could ever imagine or guess or request in your wildest dreams! He does it not by pushing us around but by working within us, his Spirit deeply and gently within us."

There is power in prayer, power in God's nearness, power in pouring out our emotions, and power in picking up His Word. "So faith comes from hearing, and hearing through the word of Christ" (Rom. 10:17 ESV).

God's Word speaks strength to wilted souls. It bolsters our believing. Press into the Word when the walls of life press in on you. Here are a few of my go-to verses in times like these:

> LORD, I have heard of your fame;
> > I stand in awe of your deeds, LORD.
> Repeat them in our day,
> > in our time make them known;
> > in wrath remember mercy....
>
> Though the fig tree does not bud
> > and there are no grapes on the vines,
> though the olive crop fails
> > and the fields produce no food,
> though there are no sheep in the pen
> > and no cattle in the stalls,
> yet I will rejoice in the LORD,
> > I will be joyful in God my Savior.
>
> The Sovereign LORD is my strength;
> > he makes my feet like the feet of a deer,

he enables me to tread on the heights.
(Hab. 3:2, 17–19)

When I said, "My foot is slipping,"
your unfailing love, LORD, supported me.
When anxiety was great within me,
your consolation brought me joy.
(Ps. 94:18–19)

My flesh and my heart may fail,
but God is the strength of my heart
and my portion forever. (73:26)

And press into prayer. Even when it's hard to pray. Even when
you want to shout to the heavens, "Come on, God! I need You here!"
Even when your prayers seem to go unanswered, or when you receive
a different answer than the one you were hoping for.

In his book *The Circle Maker*, Mark Batterson said,

The hardest thing about praying hard is enduring
unanswered prayers. If you don't guard your heart,
unresolved anger toward God can undermine faith.
Sometimes your only option is trust because it is
the last card in your hand, but it's the wild card. If
you can trust God when the answer is no, you're
likely to give Him praise when the answer is yes.
You need to press in and press on.[3]

There is never a time when God doesn't hear the cries of His children.

Believe it. He hears your prayers and can be trusted.

When we press past the pain in prayer, when we press into Jesus, peace sutures bleeding hearts and holds them tenderly until they heal. Agony is attended to by the One who knows the wrenching sting of pain, betrayal, and loss. By the One who understands. The compassionate One who reaches for the trembling hands of a struggler, picks her up, and carries her to a place of wholeness and healing. He fights for His child when she is too weary and worn to engage in the battle (Exod. 14:14).

Though the walls press in, God is able and available to work within—deeply and gently—with a grace that gives strength and is sufficient for your every need.

Yes. Doubts will come ... but God will meet you in your doubts and walk you toward faith.

Believe. Make that choice. Then wait in expectation of the God you know.

POSITIONED TO RECEIVE GOD'S POWER

You've got this, friend. Access to all the power God has for you. Let's revisit what you can do to position yourself to receive His power.

When you fear God, ask God, and seek godly counsel, you'll find the treasures of wisdom that are hidden in Christ.

When you allow the Holy Spirit to connect your life dots, He will lead you to a maturity that is firmly rooted in strength.

When you live with your eyes wide open to the beautiful and are intentional, you will find rest from your weary in God's presence. As you reflect, engage, surrender, and trust, He will equip you for whatever comes your way.

And when you pray with a heart that's willing to get down and dirty in deep confession, when you extend God an invitation to use you, and when you expect big things from our above-and-beyond God, you position yourself in the center of His power through Christ.

Lord Jesus, be the center ... because we want it all!

FOR YOUR REFLECTION AND RESPONSE

- List a few of your ungodly behaviors that diminish the power of God in your life.
- What would it look like if you were to give God total access to your life?
- Spend a few moments in prayer. Confess any sins you've been reluctant to address, and pluck out each stray one by one.
- Think of a time when the Lord allowed you to participate in the work He was doing in the life of another. Journal about it and give Him thanks for including you.
- What big things are you expecting God for today? (Tweet your answer to me @GwenSmithMusic using #iwantitall or leave a comment on my Facebook wall.)

Part 3

ALL THE IMPACT

Chapter Eleven

HIS EYE IS ON MORE THAN JUST THE SPARROW

The Bible's message is that you matter to God. Our
response is that God should matter to us.

Dillon Burroughs

One day a few years back, I dropped my kids off at school, swung into the local gas station, and ran inside to prepay. I handed the cashier forty dollars and then headed out the door to pump my gas. As I left the minimart, I recognized a woman coming in the door—the secretary for a local church. We chatted for a few minutes and then each went about our days.

My next stop? The coffee shop.

I grabbed a piping hot dark roast, added a happy little splash of half-and-half, and settled down with my Bible and journal for some one-on-one time with the Lord. In the hour and a half that followed, I read, prayed, and chatted with a few friends who came through the shop. It was a peaceful, pleasant morning … until a horrible realization hit me full force: I never pumped my forty dollars' worth of gasoline!

Oh. My. Glory.

I had pulled up to the gas pump, paid the cashier in cash, and then *driven away!* And, no … I didn't have a receipt to prove that I had paid.

This wasn't good.

Immediately my self-talk went something like this: *How can you be so dumb, Gwen? You can't even do simple things right! If you mess up on little things like this, how can you expect to do bigger things?*

In a flash I was out the door and on my way back to the gas station. I felt like such a ding-dong. I prayed the whole way there, *Please, Lord, let the same cashier still be working. Please let her remember me!*

I screeched into the parking lot on two wheels (kidding), ran inside, and blurted out, "Do you remember me?" The cashier turned to me with a smile and a receipt in her hand and said, "I know exactly who you are! You're paid in full. Go ahead and fill up!"

I thanked her profusely and breathed a big sigh of relief.

As I pumped my gasoline, the panic faded to peace. In that moment the Lord spoke to my heart as if to say, *Hey, Gwen! I know you too. Rest in My love. You are Mine, designed by My hands. Each time you turn to My heart and My Word, My response is the same. I love you … cherish you. Not because you do everything right but because you are My precious daughter. Just like the cashier, I know exactly who you are! You are paid in full. Go ahead and fill up!*

Oh how I needed that reminder that I matter and have value. Because I may look confident and put together on the outside (when

I'm not in my yoga pants or forgetting to pump the gas I paid for!), but on the inside I often wander back to that little girl who questions her value and wants to make a difference.

There are lots of ways this inner struggle presents itself in me …

- I tether my value to how I look.
- I tether my value to how my jeans fit.
- I tether my value to how I perform.
- I want my husband and kids to love me perfectly, even though they can't.
- I want to love others perfectly, but I don't, so I juggle guilt like a hot potato.
- I get distracted and waste time, so I feel unproductive.
- I want to make a difference, but I try to do too much.

The Bible showcases a perfection that I implement pathetically. Like that love chapter in 1 Corinthians that most of us had read at our weddings. Verses like "love is patient and kind; love does not envy or boast; it is not arrogant or rude. It does not insist on its own way" (13:4–5 ESV). Wait, what? Geez! The way I love doesn't even come close to this list! And then the big left hook smacks me hard: "Love never fails" (v. 8). The magnitude of God's perfect love is epic. The magnitude of my love is minuscule.

I *try* to be patient. I *try* to be kind. I *try* not to envy or boast. All of it. But my efforts are less than. I stub my toe on my ego all the time. I get edgy and loud. I insist on my own way. And then I beat myself up! *If I were a better mom, I would've ____. If I were a better friend, I would____. If I were in better shape, then maybe ____. If I were more talented, I would be able to ____.* And because I'm not content with my own body, my own behaviors, and my own abilities, I struggle to see how a perfect God can look past my brokenness. I know in my heart that He loves me, but I sometimes struggle to accept that He *likes* me, because sometimes I don't even like myself.

These doubts and insecurities cause me to question my value and my ability to make a difference. They cause me to feel insignificant. Invisible and ineffective.

Yet I know that the Bible says the opposite. And because of this, I'm reminded to, instead, tether my value to truths like these:

- I was created in the image of God.
- I am sealed with the Holy Spirit.
- Jesus loved me so much that He endured a horrific death so I could be saved.

These truths matter. And because they matter, they confirm to me that *I* matter. And they confirm that you matter too.

Don't think for one little minute that I don't sense you bristling up. It's what we girls do when the spotlight of attention is shined on our significance. We shy away. Throw our hands up to shield the light. Contest with our best excuses …

Some of us contend, *I'm really nothing special. That word* valuable *makes me nervous. My life is less than. Average at best. Mac and cheese is my jam. I drive a minivan, wear ponytails, use off-brand detergent, and live paycheck to paycheck. Where is the value in that?*

Others of us contend, *I cannot believe you're going to go there! Did you not read my bumper sticker and T-shirt? I am nothing. Jesus is everything. Hide me in the cross and stop trying to make me feel special. Slap! Slap! Slap! Shame on you for even bringing up such a topic of the flesh!*

Some of us acquiesce: *Okay. Let's talk. I know in my mind that I'm precious to Jesus, but that often gets lost in translation on its way to my heart. Yes. Let's have this conversation. I want everything God has for me, and I'm ready to move forward as a woman of greater impact.*

Wherever you find yourself in these responses, my prayer is that you will join our last friend with an expectant and curious heart. With a heart that is ready to move forward in the truth of your significance so that you can live out the purpose for which you were created.

In this final section of our "I want it all" journey, we're going to explore a few of the ways you and I can be women of exceptional impact. In this chapter we'll look at how understanding our value and our purpose to be an imprint of Christ affects the influence we have on those around us.

YOU. HAVE. VALUE.

Perhaps at this point in the book—the impact section—you're expecting me to talk about what you can *do* for God. Do. Do. Do. We love to do things, don't we? But the harder—and better—thing is for us to go street level and heart level about who we are to God and search the Scriptures to see why this matters in the grand scheme of God's purpose for our lives.

When it comes to knowing the value God places on us, I like to turn to Jesus's comments about sparrows. Do you know much about these little birds? They're a dime a dozen. Highly common. Highly overlookable. The way many of us women might feel on any given day.

Look at what Jesus had to say in reference to both ordinary little sparrows (and you):

> Are not five sparrows sold for two pennies? Yet not one of them is forgotten by God. Indeed, the very hairs of your head are all numbered. Don't be afraid; you are worth more than many sparrows. (Luke 12:6–7)

In Matthew's version of that same illustration, Jesus tacked on an additional statement: *Not one of those tiny birds can fall to the ground apart from the will of God* (Matt. 10:29, paraphrase). Apart from the will of God, not even a common, little, plain-Jane sparrow can fall to the ground.

For context, Luke 12:1 tells us that Jesus was addressing "a crowd of many thousands" when He spoke of the value God sees in each person. *Many* thousands. The rich. The poor. The average. The misfits. The bland. The spicy. The employed. The unemployed. The talented. The crippled. The lonely. The well. The sick. The married. The widowed. The single. The stressed-out. The curious. The masses! This wasn't just a pat on the back to encourage His besties! He was talking to the gamut of humanity. This is important because it makes the words He spoke that much more amazing.

Think about what He said! "You know those sparrows that are sold in the marketplace for next to nothing? Those overpopulated little flyers? My Father doesn't forget even one of them! He remembers them all."

You know what this means, don't you?

He remembers and sees you too.

You. Have. Value.

You are not forgotten by God. He sees everything about you—even your screwups and failings and fears and doubts—and He finds value. I don't love my children any more or less because of the way they dress or because of how well they can sing, throw a football, play chess, or pray publicly. God doesn't love you and me any more or less because of what we can or cannot do, or because of how good or bad we are either. He loves us because we are His. Made in His image. Fashioned by His heart. Believe it. Even if your life wasn't planned in the heart of your parents, it was planned in the heart of God. You are His, and He remembers you. By name.

You, me, and the stars. He knows us all *by name*: "He determines the number of the stars; he gives to all of them their names" (Ps. 147:4 ESV).

God knows you. He's mindful of you!

David couldn't help but respond to the wonder of God's intimate love for us:

> O Lord, our Lord,
>   how majestic is your name in all the earth!
> You have set your glory above the heavens....

When I look at your heavens, the work of your
fingers,
the moon and the stars, which you have set in
place,
what is man that you are mindful of him,
and the son of man that you care for him?
(Ps. 8:1, 3–4 ESV)

God cares for you, and He knows all about you. He knows how you like your coffee. He knows your weaknesses and insecurities. He knows all of the things that make you unique, even if you're an identical twin! He knows the things that make you tick, the quirky things, the things that cause you to beat yourself up, and the things that put a fire in your belly. And He knows how many hairs are on your head. Incredible!

And Jesus didn't stop there. He looked those people eyeball to eyeball and told them, *You … and you … and you … and you … and you … and you … are worth more than a whole mess of sparrows!*

God really *is* that into you.

Because you are His. Handcrafted with divine devotion.

I can't help but notice that before Jesus told the people how valuable they were to God, He said, "Don't be afraid" (Luke 12:7).

Don't be afraid? Why would Jesus say that?

I wonder if it was because He knows that many of us are afraid that our lives don't matter. We fear insignificance. We worry that our contributions are dumb, weak, and worthless. I wonder if it was because He sees beyond the prodigal to the potential, and He wants us to stop listening to those other voices and let Him—our Creator—tell us our value.

And I wonder if some of us might be afraid of God's love. Afraid to be defined by His grace. Afraid to be refined by His holiness … to be set free, because those old chains that bind and hinder are our normal.

Jesus made it clear: In God's eyes, you are of great value. You are loved, cherished, seen, and adored.

No one understands the insecurities of a woman like another woman. I'm with you in the battle, friend. I've wasted a fair amount of time searching for significance in the approval of others and of God. This struggle looks different in each season of a woman's life. A college student might search for validation in her sorority or GPA, a young mom has to fight to find her importance in stinky diaper changes and 3:00 a.m. feedings, while an empty nester or single woman might seek to have her value esteemed by leading a Bible study or volunteering, or in a nip and a tuck.

The secret to finding our significance is knowing God's heart for us. Once we understand that we are significant to Him, we can move forward in the purpose He has for us—because every life has a purpose.

YOUR PURPOSE = AN IMAGE BEARER

Let's rewind humanity's story way back to the beginning. "Then God said, 'Let us make man in our image, after our likeness.' … So God created man in his own image, in the image of God he created him; male and female he created them" (Gen. 1:26–27 ESV).

My brain doesn't know what to do with this. I don't know how to process this mystery. His image displayed in my life. How can that be? How can there be such a compelling connection between God's heart and my humanity? Especially when I know me. I know that on my best, most holy day, I don't come close to being *imago Dei,* the image of God.

Even so, the Bible says that I am made in God's image (v. 27), and that Jesus is the "radiance of the glory of God and the exact imprint of his nature" (Heb. 1:3 ESV). As followers of Jesus, you and I get to share in the glory of God and reflect His nature as well. The apostle Paul wrote it this way:

> And we all, with unveiled face, beholding the glory of the Lord, are being transformed into the same image from one degree of glory to another. For this comes from the Lord who is the Spirit. (2 Cor. 3:18 ESV)

Be an Imprint

When I think about what it means to leave God's imprint on the world, I'm reminded of the signet ring my mother used to wear. When I was a little girl, I loved looking at my mom's hands. Her fingers were elegant, long, and slender. On her left hand she wore a simple gold wedding band that was eight millimeters thick. No diamond, just the band. And on her right hand, she wore a gold signet ring she got when she was eighteen. I always wanted a wedding ring and a signet ring just like hers.

The signet ring had a monogram of her surname: *A* for Adams, not *E* for Eisaman (her married name). The ring seemed to be a bridge of sorts that connected who she was to who she is. I loved that. Loved that my mom's two hands wore two symbols that represented the spectrum of her identity. She grew up an Adams and will always be an Adams. She married an Eisaman and became an Eisaman. Her signet ring left me with an impression that echoed the importance of her identity.

I did some research and learned about the following parallels between signet rings and what it means to be God's imprint:

- Signet rings were used for a purpose: to authenticate a letter or message. Christ followers are used to bring God glory as we authenticate the hope of Christ to the world. Jesus said, "This is to my Father's glory, that you bear much fruit, showing yourselves to be my disciples" (John 15:8).

- Signet rings were used to leave an imprint, a distinct impression that validated that the message being delivered was genuine. Jesus kicked it up a few notches for His followers by telling us that our love for one another authenticates our faith. He was talking to His disciples when He said, "A new command I give you: Love one another. As I have loved you, so you must love one another. By this everyone will know that you are my disciples, if you love one another" (13:34–35).

Do you see? You and I are signets for the King of Kings. We are to bear evidence of the message of His hope—no matter what compromising assignment our bosses give us, no matter what carrot of temptation is dangled before us, no matter what argument that person tries to bait us into, no matter *what* lions' dens we might be thrown into. We're called to "always be prepared to give an answer to everyone who asks you to give the reason for the hope that you have. But do this with gentleness and respect, keeping a clear conscience, so that those who speak maliciously against your good behavior in Christ may be ashamed of their slander" (1 Pet. 3:15–16).

To fulfill our purpose as image bearers, we not only need to be an imprint; we also need to "rep the house" well. What does that mean? Read on.

Repping the House

Ever since our kids were little, Brad and I have taught them that the Lord is the head of our home, and every Smith needs to rep the house well. The rules are simple: Love God. Love others. Use your manners. Use kind words. Wear clean underwear. Say please. Say thank you. Say you're sorry. Be a helper. Get the door for people. Work hard. Go out of your way to make other people feel special.

And our kids know that Brad and I are always around to give them a "Good job, kid!" We expect them to rep the house. We reward them when they do and hold them accountable when they don't.

As children of the holy, loving King of Kings, you and I need to recognize our value in the big picture of God's kingdom—"the eyes of the LORD search the whole earth in order to strengthen those whose hearts are fully committed to him" (2 Chron. 16:9 NLT). And we need to rep the house ... to be the imprints that authenticate and validate the reality of God's grace.

When I think of a woman who knew her value and purpose—and who repped the house well, I think of Gertie. She was a woman of eternal impact.

To me she was Grandma Eisaman, and she lived right across the street when I was a young girl. She was famous in our small town for her engaging personality and baking skills. Her specialties? Pineapple-upside-down cake, cinnamon sticky buns, and apple dumplings that were served piping hot in a bowl à la mode. (I just drooled on my computer.) She was *most famous*, however, for her homemade bread. Breathe deeply and smell it with me. It was melt-in-your-mouth magic.

When she was just fifty-eight years old, Grandma had a massive stroke that paralyzed the left side of her body. Life was hard after the stroke. Getting around took a good deal of effort. Grandma's face didn't look the same. It drooped on one side. Her body didn't cooperate. I'm sure that was frustrating. Her life pace had to slow down.

Grandma lived the final five years of her life disabled, and yet she chose not to be defined by her limitations. Over time she learned to walk with a cane and even relearned how to drive her car (with a few modifications). How cool is that?

And she went on living. She continued to play bridge with her friends, was a leader at her church—and kept on baking. Though her life took an unexpected and challenging turn, Grandma Eisaman continued to laugh, bless, and serve others at church, in the community, and in the kitchen by baking and giving away countless loaves of fresh-baked, homemade bread.

Grandma Eisaman didn't allow her challenges, insecurities, and limitations to define her value or purpose. She knew who she was in the eyes of her Creator, and she knew that she was put on earth to be His imprint. In sickness and in health. With a vibrant, youthful smile in her younger years, and with the crooked, partially paralyzed smile she wore after her stroke.

What happens when a woman embraces both her value and her purpose? She is satisfied in her significance because she knows that God, and God alone, defines her value. She is resilient through hard times to work out God's plan for her to be an intentional imprint of His image to the world, and she reps the house well.

We are more than our health. We are more than our abilities. We are more than who other people say we are. We are more than our doubts and insecurities lead us to believe. We are women of value who bear the image of Christ and are purposed to be an imprint of His hope to the world. To authenticate Jesus. If you and I can walk in the truth of this call, we'll bring glory to God as women of impact.

And if we can bake awesome homemade bread too … all the better!

FOR YOUR REFLECTION AND RESPONSE

- Name a few of the doubts about your value or significance that you sense the Lord is leading you to move beyond.
- How does knowing that God knows you and considers you valuable—the fact that He sees you and knows your name—affect the way you perceive yourself? How should it affect the way you perceive yourself? Why should this matter?
- What behaviors do you display that might hinder you from being God's imprint to the people in your life?
- What are a few practical ways you can be an imprint of God to your family, friends, and coworkers? (Tweet your answer to me @GwenSmithMusic using #iwantitall or leave a comment on my Facebook wall.)

Chapter Twelve

STICKS AND STONES AND SALUBRIOUS TONES

*The magic of words is that they have power to do more
than convey meaning; not only do they have the power
to make things clear, they make things happen.*

Frederick Buechner

Several summers ago I flew to Nashville to record vocals for a CD project. My friend Kerri and I had spent the last day of my trip in a studio recording background vocals. When we were finished, I had to hightail it to the airport to catch my flight home.

Kerri sweetly offered to take me. As we made our way to her vehicle, she mentioned that her young daughter had dropped a sippy cup in her car the day before, and she hadn't been able to locate it. Then she said, "She was drinking milk, so there's just no telling what my car is going to smell like!"

"No problem," I shrugged. "I'm a mom. I've dealt with many a missing sippy cup in my day. How bad can it be?" (You know where this is going, don't you?)

Did I mention that it was one of the hottest days in August? Yep. It was.

As we opened the car doors, Kerri and I were smacked silly with the stinky smell of sour milk. Not just a subtle smell, mind you, but a dominant, been-sitting-in-the-hundred-degree-weather-all-day smell. The car reeked something fierce! We laughed until we almost cried at how horrible it smelled as we made our way down the expressway to the airport.

My point? Smells matter. Some smells, like the stink of sour milk, are offensive. They make you want to run and hide. While other smells, like fresh-baked cinnamon buns or a lotioned-up baby, are awesome and inviting.

I've come to realize that the words we speak affect others as much as smells do. Maybe more. Words can make others want to be near us or want to run and hide from us. While positive, constructive, and productive comments build others up and please God, negative and destructive words tear down and dishonor God.

We get provoked or irritated, and we react without a filter. We share opinions that are flesh-led instead of Spirit-led. We suck the air out of the room with tones of disgust, anger, disapproval, or sarcasm. We talk about other people, bend the truth, and point fingers. Ungodly talk can weaken relationships to frailty and is as offensive to the Lord as stinky, sour milk is to us.

Until we find the sippy cup and get it out of the car, the car still stinks.

Until we identify the destructive words we speak and expel them from our vocabulary, our conversations will continue to stink, and we won't experience the love, joy, and peace in our homes and relationships that we long for.

I polled a few friends about the stinky things they say to their loved ones, phrases they want to stuff back into their mouth as soon as they say them. Here are a few of their answers.

- "What's wrong with you?"
- "Shut up!"
- "Am I the only one who can do anything right?"
- "Idiot. How could you be so dumb?"
- "Your teammate played terrible today! What was her problem?"
- "There is no way you love me, because you …"
- "Stop being so lazy!"
- "If you stopped acting like a child, I wouldn't treat you like one!"
- "Did you hear what Mark said to Jenny?"
- "You always …! You never …! Why can't you ever …?"

Have you ever let any phrases like these fly out of your mouth? I have. Why do we say harmful things like this? Negative and harsh words are toxic because they don't leave room for grace or truth to grow. When a woman who loves Jesus speaks careless or sinful words, she wounds her own heart as much as the heart of that other person. She cringes inside. She wallows in regret. She stews in anger. She struggles to sleep and find joy. She wonders why her self-control is so lame and her tongue is so wild. And she hates it. She hates the words she spews and the tones she uses.

What would happen if we defied our sass and began to move toward becoming women who use their words to speak life, to build bridges, and to restore relationships that are weak or torn down? What kind of impact could those types of conversations have?

As I began to investigate ways to have a positive impact with my words, I came across a new word that I'm a good bit gaga about: *salubrious*. It's an adjective that means "health-giving or healthy." Don't you love that? Say it aloud a few times. Salubrious. Salubrious. Salubrious. (You're welcome.)

I want my words to be salubrious. I want them to be as inviting as the wafting fragrance of that candle shop at the mall. I want them to be life-giving. I want to use my words and my tone of voice to bless people and love them well. Isn't that what we all want? Isn't that what pleases God? To be clear: I'm still a work in progress when it comes to this, but by God's grace I *am* making progress.

My heart is hushed as I reflect on the way the apostle James addressed the importance of our words in the New Testament:

> My dear brothers and sisters, take note of this:
> Everyone should be quick to listen, slow to speak
> and slow to become angry, because human anger
> does not produce the righteousness that God
> desires.... Those who consider themselves religious
> and yet do not keep a tight rein on their tongues

deceive themselves, and their religion is worthless.
(James 1:19–20, 26)

I know this verse. Maybe you do too. Maybe you even know
it by heart or have it written on an index card that's taped to your
bathroom mirror. But as James reminds us not so subtly, knowing
and doing are two different things (v. 22). It isn't good enough for us
to be "knowers" of God's Word. If we want to be women of great and
godly impact, we must also be doers.

So let's break down these verses so we can better implement
what they have to say about how to ensure that our words will be
salubrious.

BE "QUICK TO LISTEN"

My girlfriend Jodie said, "This is difficult for a girl who likes to finish
sentences and finds silence to be the most uncomfortable sound in the
world. I often have to turn off the voice in my own mind to really hear
the other person." I get her. Don't you? Such good advice. To be a good
listener, I have to turn off the voice in my mind. I don't need to think
of my answer while the other person is talking; I need to listen and be
in the moment. I need to hear. When I hear, I'm better equipped to be
compassionate, understanding, gracious, and honorable.

I get myself in trouble when I don't listen. I stumble over arrogant thoughts, confident that I know more, understand more, have
a better idea, a more correct idea, or a holier idea. God knew this
would be a struggle for most of us. He points us to a better way in
His Word. Be quick to listen.

BE "SLOW TO SPEAK AND SLOW TO BECOME ANGRY"

This may come as news to some of you, but I have lots of opinions. Gobs of them! And I have almost convinced myself that people need to hear them. Certainly my husband. He should know where I stand on everything he says and everything he thinks. Right? And my kids?

"Oh, my kids *love* when I give them my opinion twenty times a day!" says no mom of teenagers … ever. So with this directive to be slow to speak, I sit up a bit straighter in my chair.

And then there is that "slow to become angry" part. Ahem! Have I mentioned that I'm a bit spicy? I credit it to being a sassy girl from the 'Burgh, but that's just a way for me to make excuses for my sin. Some people hold their anger in. I'm not that kind of people. My anger becomes a lovely fireworks display inside our home. Light my fuse, and I'll show you some sparkling colors and allow you to hear my booms!

And with that vulnerable gem of an admission, we move on to the next oh-so-challenging point and then on to a new process that will lead us toward the righteousness God desires from us.

"KEEP A TIGHT REIN ON YOUR TONGUE"

The apostle Paul told the believers in Ephesus, "Do not let any unwholesome talk come out of your mouths, but only what is helpful for building others up according to their needs, that it may benefit those who listen" (Eph. 4:29). One important word to notice in that verse is the word *any*. Dang, Paul! That doesn't even leave room for a loophole or an excuse that starts with "But *he* said ..."

You and I may have a word-choice problem, but it doesn't have to have us! We are children of God who are filled with His righteousness. It's time for a new day with words, girlfriend. Chin up. Shoulders back. Deep breath. Intentional step forward. It's time to get a bit more hands-on about how we can ensure that our words are life-giving.

Choose Words That Pass the KUT Test

I've come up with a little three-question tool that will help even the spiciest individual speak words that honor God, benefit others, and build them up according to their needs. Before you speak, make sure your words make the KUT:

1. Are they kind?
2. Are they useful?
3. Are they true?

Obviously this isn't an exhaustive list of guidelines, but it's a great, easy-to-remember tool that can help train us to have a biblical mind-set as we learn to be positive and productive in our conversations. The KUT Test helps to sift out words of anger, hurt, negativity, rudeness, arrogance, prejudice, ignorance, and foolishness. And so much more! It's like a Brita filter for your mouth! I'd call that productive, wouldn't you?

Let's explore a bit more how you can be sure that your words are salubrious.

1. Are My Words Kind?

Who doesn't like a kind word? We all do. So before you speak, ask yourself, "Is what I'm about to say kind?" If your words will unrighteously ruffle someone's feathers, then it's better not to speak them. (There *are* times when words need to ruffle feathers. True enough. But they should still be kind, constructive, and God honoring.)

When we speak kind words, even fussy hearts begin to untangle. Look what Proverbs has to say about kind words:

- "A gentle answer will calm a person's anger, but an unkind answer will cause more anger" (15:1 NCV). Kind words calm anger. Note to self: don't stir the pot.

- "When she speaks, her words are wise, and she gives instructions with kindness" (31:26 NLT). Kind words also give instruction.

- "Anxiety weighs down the heart, but a kind word cheers it up" (12:25). Kind words lift heavy hearts.

If what I'm about to say is unkind, then it fails the KUT Test, and I zip my lip. No talky. If what I'm about to say is kind, I can then proceed to the next step in the KUT Test.

2. Are My Words Useful?

My nerves were raw because of the faint, repetitive sound in the background of our conversation. As I sat in my parents' kitchen talking to my mom, the faucet behind her was dripping ... and dripping ... and dripping.

Drove me bananas.

I got up and tightened the handle.

It didn't help.

I wanted to grab the nearest screwdriver and fix it. But I couldn't. I'm not a sink fixer. I can't express to you how severely lacking my sink-fixing skills are. And although I'm sure there is an online instructional video that could teach me how to fix that faucet in five quick steps, I had neither the desire to learn nor the patience to try.

Drip. Drip. Drip.

Isn't it amazing how something so small and insignificant can bother us? It was torture! I left the room. I had to. I needed to get away from the sound of the drip.

Once I composed myself, I got to thinking. The Bible compares this type of drip to a quarrelsome and nagging woman. *The Message* paraphrase of Proverbs 27:15 reads, "A nagging spouse is like the drip, drip, drip of a leaky faucet; you can't turn it off, and you can't get away from it." And in the New International Version, Proverbs 19:13 says, "A quarrelsome wife is like the constant dripping of a leaky roof."

The word *nag* is defined by *Merriam-Webster Online Dictionary* this way:

- to find fault incessantly: complain
- to be a persistent source of annoyance or distraction
- to irritate by constant scolding or urging

Zinger!

Obviously this behavior isn't gender specific; men can surely nag and be quarrelsome too. Whether the behavior comes from a man or a woman, a friend or a foe, the impact is universal: nagging drives people to frustration, pushes them away, and does not bring glory to God.

I wonder how many times we drive coworkers, husbands, children, friends, or even acquaintances away because of our nagging or quarrelsome behavior? Are we even aware of when we're being nags? Do we justify our nagging when another person fails to meet our expectations?

Am I stepping on some toes here? I assure you, mine are bearing the weight too. Oh how we can complain and vie for control. Our expectations of others can stir us up. We think we know how they should act, communicate, behave, respond, and dress. The truth of the matter is, we cannot choose behavior for others, but we can choose for ourselves.

We can choose to walk worthy of our calling in Christ (Col. 1:10). We can choose to call on God so that His Spirit can be evidenced in and through us in the spiritual discipline of self-control. Nagging fuels the fire of contention and frustration. Quarreling does the same.

But don't take my word for it; take God's Word for it! "As charcoal to embers and as wood to fire, so is a quarrelsome person for kindling strife" (Prov. 26:21).

So you see? There's a snag in our nag! We can try to justify nagging all we want, but when push comes to shove, it isn't a behavior that Scripture supports. Say it with me, "There's a snag in my nag!"

In light of this, what will your behavior look like next time you're tempted to nag, quarrel, complain, or control another person? Here are a few ideas I came up with to help me speak words that are useful:

- **Replace nagging with prayer.** Not with *Lord, change him or her!* But with *Lord, change me. Help me. Strengthen me. Give me Your grace. Give me Your wisdom.*

- **Leave the room or conversation if possible or appropriate.** Don't even give yourself a chance to get harmful words out! Get away.

- **Change what you can control: your response.** "Do everything without complaining and arguing, so that no one can criticize you. Live clean, innocent lives as children of God, shining like bright lights in a world full of crooked and perverse people" (Phil. 2:14–15 NLT). Complaining and arguing aren't useful. If the Bible warns against these two behaviors, then I've got to conclude that they fall into the *no-go* category.

When my buttons are pushed, I have several choices. I can choose to be sassy and destructive. I can choose not to respond and engage in the argument. Or I can choose to respond in kindness that has the potential to calm a flustered heart. See? Lots of options. But my best choice is to pray first and *then* choose my response. Even just a whispered prayer, *Lord, please give me Your wisdom and grace for this moment! Filter my words and calm my heart.*

I reach for His calming and move to the next step as I consider my response options.

3. Are My Words True?

Let me jump on this one right away with a qualifier: Just because something is true does not mean it's wise to say. Here's why. What I have to say might be true, but if it's neither kind nor useful, then—in most cases—it doesn't need to be said. So truth isn't reason enough to say something.

The Bible says that our words are to "benefit" those to whom we speak (Eph. 4:29). Truth must be spoken in light of both wisdom and grace. We've talked about both of these imperatives on our "I want it all" journey, so prayerfully consider what you've learned in previous chapters as you apply the KUT Test.

Jesus prayed that God would sanctify us in His truth, which is the Word of God (John 17:17). And that, friend, is the best thing for us when it comes to our words. Our words need to be sifted through God's truth. If what we're about to say doesn't line up with Scripture, then we simply shouldn't say it.

"That haircut makes her look ten pounds heavier."

"That man is totally obnoxious."

"I wish you made more money so I could ..."

And would it be against the rules for me to swing back around to that other t word: tone? Would you allow me that grace? If I can't say something that is kind, useful, and true without a sarcastic or unloving tone, then it's better that I not speak. Our tones matter too, because they reflect our hearts. Amen? Amen.

I want to be a woman who speaks with life-giving words of wisdom. I want to be a woman who builds others up. I want my life to speak the hope of Christ ... to speak the truth with grace.

Eventually my parents got their leaky faucet fixed. I'm still working on my leaky lips, but with God's help, I know I can be a woman who uses her words wisely.

Are you beginning to see that you can too? Let's pray.

Lord, I really need Your help with this one. I want all of my conversations to be positive and constructive, led by Your kindness, useful and true. Please help me be quick to listen, slow to speak, and slow to anger. Help me keep a tight rein on my tongue so that the words I choose to speak reflect Your righteousness. 'Cause, Lord, I want every opportunity to impact the people in my life toward You. In Jesus's name, amen.

FOR YOUR REFLECTION AND RESPONSE

- Let me ask you something: If your words gave off a smell, how would you smell today? This past week? This past month?
- In this chapter I listed some stinky things we say that don't pass the KUT Test. What are a few of the phrases that fly from your lips that aren't kind, useful, or true?
- Spend a few moments in prayer asking God to help you honor Him with your words and eliminate those specific phrases from your vocabulary.
- Which of the three steps in the KUT Test do you think will be most helpful for you to implement? Why? (Tweet your answer to me @GwenSmithMusic using #iwantitall or leave a comment on my Facebook wall.)

Chapter Thirteen

THE GREATNESS GAMES

When we admit we are least, we feel like the greatest.
And when we lose our lives, we find it all ... all the
love, all the life, all the thrill, all the fulfillment.

Jen Hatmaker, *Interrupted*

In my spare time I help coach our high-school volleyball team. Let me rephrase that, because I do *not* have spare time. Three months a year I choose to invest daily in the lives of young female athletes who play volleyball at the high school where my children attend.

One of the games we play in practice is called Queen of the Court, the goal of which is simple: Gain and keep the lead. Dominate. Be the best and protect your turf at all costs. Serve more aggressively, pass more accurately, set more strategically, and hit harder than your opponents. It's a fast-paced drill of skill. Only the strong survive.

My life sometimes feels like a game of Queen of the Court. I strive, set goals, create a game plan, and execute the strategy. I long to be my best (a good thing), but at times my goal changes from wanting to experience all of God's best for me to wanting to be *the* best (not so good). *"Look at me, everyone! Check out my people, my position, my possessions, my trophies of greatness."*

I have to check my heart.

Am I striving to be my best in order to make the most of what God has given me … or because I want to impress others and be at the top of the heap? Those are two very different questions.

Too often I become fixated on aggressively spiking balls on the volleyball court of my ego, my family, my church, my community, my country. (My goodness!) To make it worse, I throw on an invisible jersey and play a game of Who Is the Greatest? against the people around me. Aren't we so good at that? We think,

- *My daughter could crush that volleyball if she could just get a good set.*
- *I would be incredible at that position if the boss would just stop giving all the best assignments to other people.*
- *If I use this decorating idea from Pinterest, my house will be the envy of every woman in the neighborhood.*

We want to be seen as the best.

We want to be the best employees, work for the biggest Fortune 500 companies, and attend the largest megachurches with the most popular pastors. We want to parent the smartest kids, serve on the most important committees, have the swankiest dogs, and dangle on the arms of hunky husbands who have a full head of hair and a six-pack. (Not Bud Light, people. *Abs.* Fab abs.)

Our shiny pursuits and performances become our social-media statuses the moment they happen. Can I get a witness? Facebook. Instagram. Twitter. We boast. We brag. We reach. We strive. We show. We want. We need.

As I think of these things, a hush falls over my heart. Conviction. Embarrassment. I feel as if I've been found out.

Because I often wrongly perceive life as being all about *me*.

Me. Me. Me.

We live in a world filled with people who are famous for being famous and consumed with the greatness of them-selfies. I'm not going to blow smoke. My last name might not be Kardashian, but on any given day, my heart can house just as much pride in how many Likes my posts and tweets get. Let me tell you a little secret: Christian pride is just as ugly as *Entertainment Tonight* pride. We Jesus girls just tend to drape it subtly over our modest-is-hottest shoulders and wear it with a smile. Because *our* sin isn't as scandalous as tabloid sin, right?

Lord, forgive us.

We all want to be great. And that's not a bad thing in and of itself. We need to be people of excellence. Jesus told a story—the parable of the talents—where He taught that each of us is responsible to wisely use what we're given (Matt. 25:14–30). God expects us to use our talents, personalities, gifts, and energy in productive ways. The problem lies in our motivation. If we're striving for excellence so that others will be oh so impressed with our accomplishments, our relationships, our homes, our sins, our service, our bank accounts, and our Bible studies, then we're acting out of pride. Instead of elevating our Lord, we're elevating ourselves.

Lord, forgive us.

The fire of conviction warms me … bends my knees.

Queen of the Court is a useful volleyball drill, but it isn't a game that Christians should be playing. It's surely not a game that I should be playing. If I really want it all, everything God has for me, all the impact He intends for me to have, then I need to be far more concerned with the greatness of God than with the greatness of Gwen.

As I get with God on these matters, He reveals some faulty ways in me and gives my heart fresh direction. In sports when you pivot, you turn to face a different direction. I realize that I need to make a plan that can help me pivot my conversations and responses toward the glory of God when I get thrown into the greatness games. Just because you and I are on an "I want it all" journey with Jesus doesn't mean this tension will disappear from our lives. Not a chance. We're constantly being invited to join in on the greatness games, and if we want to be women of eternal impact, we need to be prepared for how we'll respond. Let's examine a three-pronged mind-set that can help us turn our conversations and responses toward the glory of God and away from ourselves. Let's unpack it.

1. BE HUMBLE

John the Baptist was the king of the greatness-of-God pivot. You know the guy. He stood out like a sore thumb. God created him and set him apart for a specific task. A great task. The greatest. To prepare the way of the Lord. A human megaphone for Jesus, John the Baptist spoke words of maximum volume as he pointed others to the One and Only and prophetically authenticated the divinity and eternal nature of Christ.

John knew who he was, and he knew who Jesus was. He was all about Jesus. Unashamedly unique, John didn't cave to comfort, popularity, expectations of others, or tradition. Instead, he walked in obedience to God and sought to make much of the Messiah.

He was an odd bird who ate some seriously unconventional food. I'm down with the honey he was fond of, but I stop way short of snacking on locusts.

Seriously.

It just wouldn't even *cross my mind* to put a big bug in my mouth for nutrition. Just saying.

And then there was his crazy fashion sense. Pretty sure his clothes caused more than a few eyebrows to rise. Camel's hair wasn't necessarily the fabric of choice for the average Hebrew man in his day. But that's what John wore.

Clearly, impressing others with his coolness wasn't John's forte or his priority. He was different. Probably not the first one picked for the dodge-ball games at Hebrew school, and he might've even got teased: "Your breath smells like stinky bugs!" Who knows? What we do know about John the Baptist is that he was born for greatness, not for average. But he didn't go about his days trying to be great. John was focused on pointing people to Jesus—not himself. He was on a sacred mission, which left others wondering about him.

The crowds wondered who he was. They wanted to know why he did the things he did. The Israelites hadn't seen a prophet in four hundred years. Something was surely up with this guy.

One day John was baptizing people in the Jordan River. The priests and Levites hounded him with questions.

Finally they said, "Who are you? Give us an answer
to take back to those who sent us. What do you say
about yourself?"

John replied in the words of Isaiah the prophet,
"I am the voice of one calling in the wilderness,
'Make straight the way for the Lord.'"

Now the Pharisees who had been sent questioned him, "Why then do you baptize if you are
not the Messiah, nor Elijah, nor the Prophet?"

"I baptize with water," John replied, "but
among you stands one you do not know. He is
the one who comes after me, the straps of whose
sandals I am not worthy to untie." (John 1:22–27)

Commissioned by God to be famous for Jesus, John had a humble
heart and perspective. "I'm not even worthy to untie this guy's sandals."
Pivot.

I love what pastor and author Dr. Tony Evans has to say about
this topic: "God is not opposed to greatness. God is opposed to
pride. Big difference. Unfortunately, it is a difference not widely
understood or embraced."[1]

Peter reminds us of this in his letter to the believers in the early
church:

All of you, clothe yourselves with humility toward
one another, because,
"God opposes the proud
but shows favor to the humble."

Humble yourselves, therefore, under God's
mighty hand, that he may lift you up in due
time. (1 Pet. 5:5–6)

Our job: be humble before God and toward others. Stop playing
the greatness game. *God's job:* to lift us up *as* He sees fit, *when* He
sees fit—all to elevate Himself. "The LORD mocks the mockers but is
gracious to the humble" (Prov. 3:34 NLT).

One way I position myself to live out this step is to welcome
accountability. My closest girlfriends and I have a deal. If they see
anything in my life that shortchanges God's glory, they have permission to tell me about it. Even if it hurts my pride. Even if it hurts my
feelings. My besties have permission to challenge me toward holiness, toward excellence in Christ. And I have permission to speak
honestly to them too. It helps to keep us humble. 'Cause let's be real
here. The tiny particles of sin dust that get into our eyes can multiply
into hardened scales of blindness quicker than you can fry an egg on
an Arizona sidewalk at midday in August.

So be humble. Next, throw a big ole Jesus party.

2. MAKE MUCH OF THE MESSIAH

Can I just say that I'm glad God didn't create me as John the Baptist?
I'd probably have been worried about the camel's-hair-and-locust
situation. I would have asked Jesus for the cute sandals I saw at Target
to protect my feet and for healthy meals and for Starbucks dark roast
to strengthen me for the task. Surely I would deserve those things.
After all, I would have been His opening act!

The greatness of the call on John's life was, in fact, all about humbly serving and directing others to Jesus. That is the greatness of the call on my life and yours too. Just like John the Baptist, we were born with a unique calling: to know God and to showcase God. To magnify His majesty.

John shows us that the secret to having all the greatness we long for is found in elevating God and making a big deal of His eminence. He turned selfish ambitions upside down when he pointed us to the paradox of the Christian faith. To be great in God's eyes, we have to get over ourselves and become the least.

The people around John started to bicker and compare his ministry to the ministry of Jesus, and they just plain stirred up trouble. "What about this law? What about that one? Why is *that guy* (Jesus) baptizing people when *you* are supposed to be the baptizer? He's taking your followers away from you! What's up with that, John?"

Trouble. Trouble. Trouble.

Have you ever been around anyone who just likes to bicker, compare you to other people, and stir up trouble? Me too. But John didn't take the bait. Here's how it went down:

> An argument developed between some of John's disciples and a certain Jew over the matter of ceremonial washing. They came to John and said to him, "Rabbi, that man who was with you on the other side of the Jordan—the one you testified about—look, he is baptizing, and everyone is going to him."
>
> To this John replied, "A person can receive only what is given them from heaven. You yourselves can

testify that I said, 'I am not the Messiah but am sent ahead of him.' The bride belongs to the bridegroom. The friend who attends the bridegroom waits and listens for him, and is full of joy when he hears the bridegroom's voice. That joy is mine, and it is now complete. He must become greater; I must become less." (John 3:25–30)

More of Him. Less of me.

Pivot.

The more I get to know Jesus, the more I come face-to-face with what I know is true: it's not about me. (And it's not about you either.) It's all about Jesus and the glory of God's greatness. You and I *were* born for greatness. Not for the world's greatness but for eternal greatness: to know God and showcase God.

John had this pivot-ready perspective because he really knew Jesus. Like *supersize, really.*

We. Need. To. Get. To. Know. Jesus. More.

The good news is He isn't hiding from us. He's findable and knowable. So I hunker down on the couch with my Bible, journal, and a willing heart. I study the Gospels. Those red-letter words that were spoken by Life about life. Those four books of the New Testament Scriptures that give an account of the life of Christ: Matthew, Mark, Luke, and John. These are a treasure chest of purest gold as I search to know my Savior more. I look at how he dealt with the people around Him, how He spoke, how He loved, and what He said. I look at His relationships, His teachings, His outreach, and His compassion.

And I pray. I worship. I meditate. I bask in the wonder of His greatness, and I set my heart in His direction. This helps me to know Him more. To grow my love for Him. And I'm reminded that spiritual growth must be a lifelong pursuit. Growing in my relationship with Jesus *is* the "I want it all" journey!

When I pause to consider who I am in light of Jesus, and when I search to know Jesus more intimately, I no longer worry about how others see me. When I live for the greatness of God, peace happens. That deep peace that makes the world scratch its head becomes the guard that protects my heart and my mind from the temptations that invite me to play the greatness game. His peace equips me to pivot. No matter who baptizes whom or whose child makes the honor roll.

3. DON'T WORRY WHERE YOU STAND IN LINE

Finally, have a mind-set that allows the Spirit of God to set the pace.

One of the things we do at dinnertime as a family is a daily recap. Simple stuff: we talk through the things that happened that day. When my kids were in elementary school, one of the first things they talked about was who got to be the line leader that day. It was a pretty big deal, especially to young Smiths who really, really loved being line leaders. (I don't know where they get that ...)

Okay, I need to be honest here. Following isn't necessarily my strong suit. I like to be in charge and in control. Especially on the road. If you and I have somewhere to go together, you might just want to let me drive, because I freak out in the passenger seat. I wonder why the invisible brake on my side never works, even when I pump it. I get frustrated with the guy in the passing lane who drives ten miles an hour *below* the speed limit and never passes anybody. It's the *passing* lane, people; therefore, pass! Clearly no one can drive as well as I can …

Hot messes. All of us!

We are so concerned with blue ribbons and lead positions.

Lord, forgive us.

Jesus showed us a better way to get where we need to go. He told His disciples to follow Him. To stop doing their own things and to do His thing. These instructions were meant for you and me as well. He wants us to do what He did—to love like He loved, to lead like He led. And He led by serving others. By humbling Himself sacrificially. He was the greatest, but He treated others as if *they* were.

In her book *Love Story*, songwriter and author Nichole Nordeman put it this way:

> Jesus sort of topples the model of traditional lead-ership. He starts at the bottom. First things first. Let's get those feet washed. This is how Jesus leads. And it's why marriages and corporations and min-istries thrive under his model of servant leadership. Stooping, not looming. Tending, not monitoring.[2]

I know this.

I really do.

I *want* this. I want this for me, and I want this for my family. I want this for you. I want to live this type of radical life that showcases Jesus and pushes His fame to the forefront. Not only on the good days but also on the bad days. Not only in the comfortable times but also in the uncomfortable, fiery times. Don't you?

JUST A GIRL IN LINE

I'm thankful that God convicts my heart when I play Queen of the Court, get bossy, start comparing, running ahead of God, or getting caught up in self-centered pursuits. His Spirit reminds me that my flesh needs to be put down because I am bound to Christ, and He is my Master. The Spirit of God reminds me that I'm not to live as a slave to sin but as a slave to righteousness (Rom. 6:15–23).

When Jesus becomes our focus, we will be in the center of God's will for us. Today, for me, this probably means I'll do more praying than social-media posting or Fox News watching. And it also means that when a certain mom bends my ear about the awesome accomplishments of her darling daughter, I'll smile, share in her joy, and *not* respond with "Well, my daughter just …"

Things go better for me when I choose humility, make a big deal of God's greatness, and follow His lead by lovingly serving the people in my life. My peace is greater when I look to the needs of others instead of my own, when I humble myself before our awesome Lord and beg for Him to be magnified in my words, thoughts, efforts, and decisions.

Jesus is the line leader.

I'm just a girl in line who needs to keep her eyes fixed on the Guy up front.

Lead, Jesus! Please lead me. Take the wheel. Take the whole car! Take my life. No more Queen of the Court for me. I want You, Jesus. I want more of You.

Amen and amen.

FOR YOUR REFLECTION AND RESPONSE

- Do you find yourself caving to comfort, competition, popularity, expectations of others, or tradition—or do you intentionally walk in obedience to God and seek to make much of the Messiah?
- How would you split the percentage of time you focus on vain pursuits versus fame-of-Jesus pursuits? What percentage would you like that to be?
- We talked about a three-prong mind-set in this chapter. Which mind-set is most challenging for you? Why?
- How can you use your social-media accounts to point your people toward the greatness of Jesus? Will you? (Tweet your answer to me @GwenSmithMusic using #iwantitall or leave a comment on my Facebook wall.)

Chapter Fourteen

WHO ME? YEAH YOU! COULDN'T BE! THEN WHO?

In all our efforts, if we are not about people, our
labors aren't really about Jesus but about us.

Brandon Hatmaker, in *Interrupted*

Growing up, my friends and I played all sorts of silly games. Fun games that connected strands of kids and tethered us to a specific time and place with a memory. One of those was the Cookie Jar game. It went like this:

Crowd: Amy stole the cookie from the cookie jar!

Amy: Who me?

Crowd: Yeah you!

Amy: Couldn't be!

Crowd: Then who?

Amy: Elise!

Crowd (redirected): Elise stole the cookie from the cookie jar!

And on and on it went, without ever getting to the heart of the matter. Sometimes I think those of us who are Jesus lovers play the Cookie Jar game when it comes to being salt and light in the world.

> **Jesus Lovers:** Susan, show the world that the Lord is good so they will be drawn to Him.
> **Susan:** Who me?
> **Jesus Lovers:** Yeah you!
> **Susan:** Couldn't be!
> **Jesus Lovers:** Then who?
> **Susan (redirected):** Tara!

And the game goes on. The directive to be salt and light keeps getting redirected to another Christian who we think has fewer chinks in her armor. This may be a silly game when it comes to cookies, but when it comes to eternal matters? Not so much. When it comes to drawing others to Christ, the "Who me?" response and redirect is a sad game.

One that I need to stop playing.

I play this game and pass up opportunities to influence others toward Christ all the time. I bow out from showcasing Him to the world—to that friend, volleyball mom, neighbor, family member, or coworker who is in desperate need of His grace. Why? Because I like my comfort. I'm betting you do too.

I have a strange sense that you might want to skip this chapter. I can almost hear you thinking, *I'm cool with Jesus. Heck, yeah! Love that Guy! I totally dig His grace, love, forgiveness, and peace. Oh ... and His comfort! Love His comfort. Love the epic lay-down-your-life and rise-again Easter thing. I am all about Jesus. But don't ask me to go talking about Him or anything. I just can't. My life is complicated. I don't know enough about the Bible. My marriage is on the fritz, I'm unemployed, and my kids are total prodigals. I can't possibly be used by God to do holy stuff.*

Am I right? Don't break up with me just yet. Because wanting all that God has for us means that we need to want what Jesus wants. To do what Jesus did. It's one of those pesky heart matters. Jesus was all about doing the will of the Father. He said, "I have come down from heaven, not to do my own will but the will of him who sent me" (John 6:38 ESV). He also told His disciples (and us) to be salt and light.

BEING SALT AND LIGHT

Jesus said,

> You are the salt of the earth, but if salt has lost its taste, how shall its saltiness be restored? It is no longer good for anything except to be thrown out and trampled under people's feet.
>
> You are the light of the world. A city set on a hill cannot be hidden. Nor do people light a lamp and put it under a basket, but on a stand, and it gives light to all in the house. In the same way, let your light shine before others, so that they may see your good works and give glory to your Father who is in heaven. (Matt. 5:13–16 ESV)

Now I'd like you to place *your name* in the following sentences: _____ is the salt of the earth. _____ is the light of the world. _____ will be given opportunities to do good works and influence others toward Jesus.

Nervous yet?

Don't be. The call to be salt and light might seem intimidating, but remember, Jesus would never ask you to do anything He wasn't going to help you with!

We're all just fumbling fools who fall more frequently than we'd like to admit. I love how author Jon Acuff broke it down:

> God found Gideon in a hole. He found Joseph in a prison. He found Daniel in a lion's den. He has a curious habit of showing up in the midst of trouble, not the absence. Where the world sees failure, God sees future. Next time you feel unqualified to be used by God remember this, He tends to recruit from the pit, not the pedestal.[1]

Bam! God recruits from the pit, not the pedestal.

You are qualified to be salt and light—in spite of your mess—because of your Messiah.

As I wade through the waters of accepting this challenge in my own life, I'm encouraged by this verse: "We are his workmanship, created in Christ Jesus for good works, which God prepared beforehand, that we should walk in them" (Eph. 2:10 ESV). I want to do what God has created me to do and walk in the ways He leads me to walk. So I committed this verse to memory. It helps to remember this when my knees go weak. God knew long ago who I would be and what good works He would place in my path. Being salt and light is the call to apply who I am in Christ in such a way that my actions would cause others, Christians and non-Christians alike, to praise God. The same is true for you.

Let this great news calm any hint of anxiousness you might be feeling right now. We get to walk in His ways with this promise:

> Such confidence we have through Christ before God. Not that we are competent in ourselves to claim anything for ourselves, but our competence comes from God. He has made us competent as ministers of a new covenant—not of the letter but of the Spirit; for the letter kills, but the Spirit gives life. (2 Cor. 3:4–6)

Being salt and light and pointing people to Jesus doesn't mean we need to start handing out Bible tracts on street corners or leaving them with a tip at the next restaurant we go to, like Uncle Bob does. It means that you and I should be open to the random God opportunities He brings our way each day, and we should intentionally bless others on His behalf.

Let me show you what I mean.

BEING OPEN TO GOD OPPORTUNITIES

Every morning I give God free rein to use me throughout the day. *Lord, please open my eyes to any way that You would like to use me today. I am willing. Place people or circumstances in my path so that by something I do, others might be encouraged toward You. In Jesus's name, amen.*

Here's an example of one such "divine appointment" the Lord allowed me to participate in. I was at the grocery store and in a rush to grab some food items so I could feed my people.

Always a rush.

A friend and I met at the corner of eggs and pretzels. Our meeting wasn't a coincidence. It was a God opportunity. I had been in a hurry and could've easily rushed past my friend's needs to fulfill my own, but God prompted me to pause. His Spirit allowed me to sense that my friend was hurting. What happened next was a Holy Spirit–directed conversation. I asked her how she was doing, and she opened up and told me of a heart wound that dripped of fear, insecurity, and doubt.

I write this not to make me look good but to make my God look good. In my flesh, I would've been way more concerned about my schedule than my saltiness. He had ordained the meeting. Both she and I knew it by the divine traces of grace, truth, and peace that covered our hearts as we said good-bye through tears and a hug.

We smiled as our carts crossed paths again at the checkout line, knowing we both came for groceries but were leaving with what we needed even more. Me: a fresh measure of gratitude and an overwhelming awe of our loving Light of the World who knows and responds to the needs of our harried hearts. Her: a personal and on-time word from God through the lips of a friend.

My heart was humbled and my thoughts soared with God's beyondness. The way He met my friend and me there. The way He rolled a shine-the-hope-of-Jesus opportunity by me in a grocery store. The way He loves her. The way He loves me. The way He loves us.

Oh how He loves us! Perfectly. Immeasurably. Personally.

The psalmist wrote, "The LORD directs the steps of the godly. He delights in every detail of their lives. Though they stumble, they will never fall, for the LORD holds them by the hand" (Ps. 37:23–24 NLT). God needed to make His love known to a discouraged daughter, and He opened my heart so that I could join Him in that beautiful mission.

Open the eyes of your heart in expectation that God may have penciled you in for a special appointment. As you remain flexible to the plans and ways of God, you'll begin to see more and more opportunities to share His love with others.

For example:

- Your new neighbor is a single mom? Watch her kids as she unpacks her boxes.
- Your coworker just had surgery? Do her laundry that week.
- Your child's teacher sounds discouraged? Listen to her heart and courageously speak God's truth in love.

You get the idea. Ask God to open your eyes to the needs around you and then take that meal, go with her to that doctor's appointment, pray with her and for her, share promises of Scripture when she is afraid.

In addition to being open to the opportunities God puts in our paths, we can be salt and light by taking initiative and being intentional.

BEING INTENTIONAL SALT AND LIGHT

Years ago I worked with a woman in Nashville named Cindy. She was a no-nonsense publisher for a major music company. Each month she listened to the songs I wrote and gave honest, constructive feedback that required this songwriter chick to have thick skin and wear big-girl panties. She was salt and light to me in the workplace, but not in ways I expected or necessarily appreciated at the time.

I didn't always love what she had to say.

Total honesty? She. Scared. Me. Silly.

I wrestled with her strong, bristly opinions, and at the same time, I grew from the pruning of her wise, professional words. She challenged me toward greater excellence, and she wasn't afraid to speak difficult words of truth.

One thing I'll never forget: as she listened to the new songs I wrote, she regularly *insisted* that I was a "worship leader/worship writer" instead of a Contemporary Christian Music (CCM) writer/artist. Drove me bananas because I was *sure* I was a CCM writer/artist.

Over the years Cindy and I became friends, and eventually I came to realize that she was right. I *am* a worship leader and worship writer. It's not only who I am; it's who I always was. Even when I didn't know it and insisted otherwise.

Cindy died in her early fifties.

Cancer stole her from us.

A few nights before she went on to be with the Lord, a large group of Nashville's finest songwriters gathered at her bedside to celebrate her life, which was salty and bright for Jesus, to thank her for her impact, to share stories, and to sacredly sing her to the other side of glory. A knot held my throat captive as I watched the gathering online via video. What a legacy. Cindy poured wisdom into so many people, she said and did things that caused others to think big thoughts about God, and she spurred them on toward excellence.

She lived a life of influence because she was intentional about being salt and light in my life and in the lives of many others.

I want to die like that.

I want to live like that.

Don't you?

In the Bible, a man named Jabez asked God for all the influence God would give him. Jabez called upon the God of Israel, saying,

> "Oh that you would bless me and enlarge my bor-
> der, and that your hand might be with me, and that
> you would keep me from harm so that it might not
> bring me pain!" And God granted what he asked.
> (1 Chron. 4:10 ESV)

Jabez wanted to live with impact to the max.

He pleaded to be a difference maker. I'm right there with him.

We all have influence. The question is, will we use our influence to sway our friends toward an awesome movie, or will we influence them toward our awesome God? Will we choose to live in a way that causes our unbelieving neighbors or coworkers to want to hear more about Jesus? Will we teach a young wife to understand how to respect her husband or help a young mom realize that God is honored when she nurtures her demanding, thankless children? Will we help the weary parent of a prodigal see that her child's rebellion isn't her failure and isn't her child's final faith chapter?

It all begins with a choice.

If we want to be women of impact, we need to live with our eyes wide open to God opportunities. We need to get beyond our own agendas and move in the direction of *His* agenda. It isn't about doing more of what we're already doing; it's about listening to the whispers of Jesus in the middle of the grocery store, or at the nail salon, in the cubicle at work, in the next pew, in the living room, or in the classroom.

Being a woman of impact isn't about doing more each day; it's about living to be led by Jesus with the days we're given.

And now it's time for us to do just that.

A FINAL POM-POM SHAKE AND A PRAYER

It has been my honor to walk through these lessons, stories, and scriptures with you. Writing this book has challenged and changed me. I hope it has done the same for you.

I want to close with a final charge. My friend, always remember this: God is with you. He loves you, is *for* you, and has a plan for you that is as exclusive as your fingerprints. He won't abandon the good work He has begun in you. He will be faithful to complete it (Phil. 1:6). It's true. Believe it.

As we say good-bye, these words written by the apostle Paul to the church of Ephesus are my heartfelt prayer for you:

> I pray that out of his glorious riches [the Father] may strengthen you with power through his Spirit in your inner being, so that Christ may dwell in your hearts through faith. And I pray that you, being rooted and established in love, may have power, together with all the Lord's holy people, to grasp how wide and long and high and deep is the love of Christ, and to know this love that surpasses knowledge—that you may be filled to the measure of all the fullness of God.
>
> Now to him who is able to do immeasurably more than all we ask or imagine, according to his power that is at work within us, to him be glory in the church and in Christ Jesus throughout all generations, for ever and ever! Amen. (Eph. 3:16–21)

FOR YOUR REFLECTION AND RESPONSE

- When was the last time you played the Christian Cookie Jar game when you had an opportunity to be salt and light?
- How could praying Jabez's prayer help you avoid playing the Cookie Jar game?
- In this chapter, we talked about the truth that Jesus will never ask you to do something that He isn't going to help you do. How does knowing this affect you? Does it make a difference? Why or why not?
- What is one practical way you could be salt and light in your sphere of influence this week? (Tweet your answer to me @GwenSmithMusic using #iwantitall or leave a comment on my Facebook wall.)

———

STUDY GUIDE

CHAPTER ONE: YOURS FOR THE ASKING

Read and Reflect

Read John 15:1–11. In verses 4 and 5, Jesus made two promises. What was He saying? Write it in your own words.

What does Jesus tell us in verse 9? What would it look like for you to remain in His love?

What did Jesus say that He wanted His disciples to experience in verse 11? What is one area of your life that you feel could use this complete Jesus joy?

Read and Reflect

Read Ephesians 3. Verse 6 says that both Jews and Gentiles (non-Jews) *are* something and *share* something. What are they, and what do they share?

What two things in verse 12 did Paul say we can approach God with? Why is this important?

What do you think Paul meant in verse 19 when he prayed that the saints would be "filled to the measure of all the fullness of God"? What would it look like for this to be true in your life?

Respond

Lord, would You fill every aspect of my life to the full so that You can be glorified in and through me? Help me to be radiant and well on both the inside and outside. Teach me to be a woman who trusts You, leans into Your power, and makes an impact for You in the lives of others. I'm ready to remain in You and to experience the fullness of Your joy as we walk this faith journey together. Let's do this, Jesus! Amen.

CHAPTER TWO: THAT THING WE NEED THE MOST

Read and Reflect

Read Psalm 36:5–7. Where does the psalmist say God's love reaches to?

How far is that? Is there an end to it?

Thank God for His unfailing love.

How far does the faithfulness of God extend? Look to the skies.

Celebrate the breadth of His love. Respond in worship.

According to these verses, how big is God's righteousness?

Have you ever been to the mountains or climbed a high hill? Consider the magnitude of it all and be swept away to the depth of His love as you acknowledge the grandeur of God's righteousness and the depth of His justice. Journal a prayer of response.

Read and Reflect

Read Ephesians 2:4–5. What was the reason God made us alive in Christ?

Read and Reflect

Read Psalm 86:15. What five words or phrases are used to describe God in this verse? How similar or different are these from the way you perceive God right now?

Respond

Dear Lord, You are perfect love … and all that my soul longs for. When I'm dizzy with discontent, please remind me that Yours is the love that satisfies. In Jesus's name, amen.

CHAPTER THREE: NOT JUST A PRAYER WE SAY BEFORE DINNER

Read and Reflect

Read Luke 15:11–31. What does this passage teach you about the plans God has for His children?

If you were an actor in a play of the lost son, would you be cast as the prodigal or the older brother? Why?

If you could speak to a younger version of your character, what would you say to her?

What are the first six words of verse 17?

These are some of my favorite words in Scripture. The lights turn on. Hope walks to center stage. The crew of workers backstage prepares to change the scenery. The music rises. God is about to run. Was there a time in your life when you "came to your senses" about your need to reconcile your relationship with God? What did that look like for you?

In verse 20, what two things did the son do?

What five things did the father do in response to the son's actions?

In verse 21, the son humbly confessed his sin against the father. What was the father's response in verses 22–24?

Was it a finger-shaking, hands-on-the-hip type of response or one of extravagant, arms-wide-open grace?

Did the son have to pay back his squandered inheritance or work his way back into the family?

What strings were attached for a celebration to take place?

How should this inform the way you view God's response to you when you humble yourself before Him?

When the older son returned from the field, what was his emotional response to the grace shown by his father (v. 28)?

How have you struggled to celebrate with someone who, in your opinion, got off the hook too easily?

How did the father perceive the difference between a found wanderer and a faithful worshipper?

Read and Reflect

Read Psalm 139. Write out the full text of verses 7–10 in your journal.

What did you notice about the presence of God as compared to the position of the worshipper?

What are the two responses of God in verse 10?

Was that in response to a worshipper who was faithful or wandering?

How does this make you feel?

Write the following sentences in your journal, filling in the blanks with your people, places, and heart matters. *Lord, Your loving presence is incredible! Your Word assures me that even if _____ happens, You are there. When I'm overwhelmed by the circumstances with _____, You are there. When I find myself filled with fears and doubts about _____, Your right hand will hold me fast. Thank You, Lord. I cherish Your presence and love You too.*

Respond

Lord, search me and know me. Show me anything in my life that needs to be refined. Shine Your holy light on any shady areas of my life that need correction or direction. Crush any stubborn ways that keep me from Your will and Your best. Magnify any secret sins or unknown compromises that hinder my holiness. Move me forward in Your grace so that I

can be led by Your Spirit and so that others can see Your love through me.
In Jesus's name, amen.

CHAPTER FOUR: CAN YOU REALLY HUG A PORCUPINE?

Read and Reflect

Read Psalm 91. Write out a few observations you saw as you read the psalm.

How do these particular observations affect you?

Look over verses 14–16 again. God is looking for three things from us. What are they?

When you and I take those three actions, what eight promises does the Lord make in response? Write them in your journal.

Read and Reflect

Read 2 Corinthians 4:16–18. Write out the first sentence in verse 16 as a personal statement of declaration.

What is the payoff for our trials that Paul talks about in verse 17?

In light of this, what does verse 18 instruct us to do and what would it look like if you did this today?

Respond

*Dear Lord, thank You for being my safety, my help, and my refuge.
When my days are full of trials and pain, I know that I can trust You
to provide the wisdom, provision, comfort, and grace I need to endure.
Help me to hug my porcupines today and to see that each challenge gives
me an opportunity to turn my eyes toward Yours and to know You more
intimately. In Jesus's name, amen.*

CHAPTER FIVE: A FAITH BEYOND FEELINGS, FAILURES, AND FEARS

Read and Reflect

Read Joshua 1:5–9. Write out three to five observations from this
passage that encourage or intrigue you.

Describe how these observations can mobilize your faith.

Read and Reflect

Read Hebrews 10:19–23. What four things are we supposed to have
as we draw near to God?

Concentrate on the first two. Write a one-sentence summary of what
each of these might look like as you approach Jesus, the new and
Living Way.

Respond

Write this paragraph in your journal and fill in these blanks: "Today I will face _____ with the courage that the Lord provides for me instead of trembling in fear. In this area of weakness, _____, I will ask God for strength and will trust that His grace is sufficient to provide what I need. And I will pray for wisdom and direction concerning _____ so that the Spirit of God can guide me with divine wisdom, which is far greater than anything I can come up with on my own."

CHAPTER SIX: BRING. IT. ON!

Read and Reflect

Read Colossians 2. What three things mentioned in verse 15 did Christ accomplish against spiritual powers and authorities on the cross?

What would it look like for you to remember these things when you face spiritual warfare?

Write out an "It is written ..." statement of this verse that you can speak confidently to the Enemy the next time you find yourself in a faith battle.

Read and Reflect

Read Ephesians 6:10–18. Why does the apostle Paul tell us to put on the armor of God?

Who is our struggle against? Who is it not against?

How should this affect the way you approach your days in prayer?

What three things does Paul tell believers to do in verse 18?

What do you think "pray in the Spirit" means?

How should these three instructions in verse 18 influence you?

Respond

Lord, thank You for the presence of Your Holy Spirit in my life. Please open my eyes wide to all the courage, strength, and wisdom You have for me in Christ. Crush my insecurities and doubts so that I might be an effective witness of Your power. I ask that You would receive the maximum amount of glory in and through my life. Please cover me in Your Spirit today and equip me to fend off attacks from the Enemy in the name of Jesus. Amen.

CHAPTER SEVEN: KEEP YOUR DIAMONDS; THIS GIRL WANTS MORE

Read and Reflect

Read Proverbs 3:13–18 ESV. Write out verses 13–15 in your journal and underline or highlight the words that are represented by blank spaces below.

"_____ is the one who finds _____, and the one who gets _____, for the gain from her is better than gain from _____ and her profit better than _____. She is _____ _____ than jewels, and _____ you _____ can compare with her."

What can you conclude from these comparisons?

List the benefits spoken of in verses 16–18 of living a life of wisdom.

Read and Reflect

Read 1 Kings 2:1–4; 3:1–15. In 1 Kings 2–3, King David taught his son Solomon that wisdom is of extreme value. He encouraged Solomon to seek after wisdom wholeheartedly, and when given the opportunity to ask anything of God, Solomon chose wisdom.

List the instructions David gave to Solomon in the first section of chapter 2, verse 3.

What did David say the result of following those instructions would be (end of verse 3)?

What do you think David meant by this?

Was he guaranteeing Solomon an easy life with no struggles if he followed the ways of the Lord? Of course not. So what do you think David did mean when he told Solomon that if he followed the ways of God, he would prosper in all he did and wherever he went?

Do you think this same promise/principle is true for you and me as followers of Christ? Why or why not?

Respond

Lord, You are holy, and powerful, and full of grace. Please forgive me for all the ways I want other things more than wisdom! Lead me in Your wisdom, knowledge, and understanding so that I can live with greater purpose and impact today. Direct my choices, my behaviors, and my heart. Forgive me for the times when I look to others or to myself when I should be looking to You. Please forgive me for my independence, arrogance, and stubbornness that keeps me from Your best, Jesus. Amen.

CHAPTER EIGHT: STAY IN YOUR OWN YARD

Read and Reflect

Read 1 Peter 5:8–9a. Write down a few observations from these verses.

How should this impact you?

Read and Reflect

Read 2 Thessalonians 3:3. What word is used to describe God?

What two action words are used to explain how He will treat you in response to His enemy?

Write a prayer of response.

Read and Reflect

Read Psalm 51. (This was David's response to his sin with Bathsheba and Uriah when Nathan the prophet confronted him in 2 Samuel 12.) What do you sense about David's heart as he wrote this psalm?

Rewrite verses 10–12 in your own words.

Take note of the turn that happens in verse 13. David trusted that his confession would bring a fresh renewal of forgiveness. What action did David say he would do in response to the restoration God brings to broken lives?

How does this compare to the call to action in Psalm 107:2?

Respond

Lord, who am I that You are mindful of me? That You know me? That You see me? That You love me? Please forgive this wandering worshipper. As I consider Your mercy, I confess these things: _____. Draw me close, once again, with Your blood-stained grace and ignite an unquenchable fire of love deep within my heart, my soul, and my mind. Please forgive me for the times I've wandered from Your plan for me and given in to temptation. Teach me Your ways. Lead me to make choices that bring You glory and allow me to experience the life You intended for me to live. Amen.

CHAPTER NINE: THE POWER OF REST

Read and REST

Read Psalm 23. Grab your journal or a piece of paper or blog it out— whatever! We're going to do a REST (Reflect, Engage, Surrender, Trust) exercise.

> **Reflect**: List three works of God's creation that you are grateful for, three ways God has provided for you

in the past, and three characteristics of God that you can reflect on in spite of your current challenges.

Engage: Write out a prayer that begins with at least three things you are grateful for and then focuses on your heart burdens that need God's rest. Be specific. Be honest. Go deep with God. (Once you give thanks and hash out the details of your challenges, move on to the next section and continue journaling.)

Surrender: *Forgive me, Lord. I am so guilty of taking matters into my own hands. I want You to lead. I need You to lead. Teach me Your ways. Empower me with Your Spirit and give me an undivided heart that I might follow close to Your Word and Your will. In Jesus's name, amen.*

Trust: Read Psalm 46:1–3. List the three ways God is described in the first verse. What would it look like for you to trust God with your biggest struggles today?

Respond

Lord, I really want to get this one! Please help me turn to You in all circumstances—in the good, the bad, and the ugly. Give me the strength to surrender my will to Yours, and guard my heart and mind with peace as I choose to trust You with my struggles today. You are awesome and strong and gracious and kind. Your goodness knows no end. When I think about the ways You have brought hope, healing, and joy to my life, I am overwhelmed with gratitude. Please help me to know You more—and to show You more—as I seek to find my rest in You. Amen.

CHAPTER TEN: WHETHER LIFE IS CALM OR COMPLICATED, DO THIS

Read and Reflect

Read Psalm 18:6. How has God been attentive and responsive to your prayers in the past?

How can and should the truth of His love for you affect your current challenges?

Read and Reflect

Read Psalm 63. Write a prayer response.

Read and Reflect

Read Hebrews 10:19–39. Write out any verses you would like to memorize or remember.

What does verse 23 tell you to do? Why?

Write out verses 38–39. What does God call the righteous to do in verse 38?

What displeases God?

Whom are we not of? How should this affect the way you approach the Lord with your prayer needs?

Respond

Lord, as they say, "The struggle is real!" Thank You for allowing me to be honest about the challenges that entangle me. Please work in my heart and in my circumstances today so that I can move forward in faith. Thank You for hearing me when I pray. Help me rest in Your love and trust Your plan. Direct my choices, my behaviors, and my heart. Forgive me for the times when I look to others or to myself when I should be looking to You. Amen.

CHAPTER ELEVEN: HIS EYE IS ON MORE THAN JUST THE SPARROW

Read and Reflect

Read Jeremiah 1:4–5. When did God first know Jeremiah?

Just as He did with Jeremiah, God thought about you and designed you before you were born. Take a few moments to read over these verses again and personalize them. How does this make you feel?

Read and Reflect

Read Daniel 6. Did you see it? How did the king seal the stone that was placed over the mouth of the den? (Hint: verse 17)

How was Daniel an image bearer of the one true God in this encounter?

Respond

Lord, help me to accept that You are the One who defines my significance. Please sift through my thoughts, doubts, insecurities, and emotions that leave me feeling like less instead of more. Thank You for always remembering me and for engraving my name on the palms of Your hands. Would You help me to be Your image bearer today? Show me practical ways to "rep the house." Amen.

CHAPTER TWELVE: STICKS AND STONES AND SALUBRIOUS TONES

Read and Reflect

Read Galatians 5:22–23. Which two fruits of the Spirit do you think God displays well in your life?

Which two fruits do you need the most help with?

Pray about those right now. Ask God to reveal any areas in your life that might not "smell" as they should.

Read and Reflect

Read Proverbs 18:21. What two powers does the tongue possess?

Which of those powers do you want your words to reflect?

What can you do today to make that happen?

Read and Reflect

Read Proverbs 16:24. Summarize this verse in your own words.

Read and Reflect

Read Colossians 3:8 and Ephesians 4:31. What emotions do you struggle with that set off these reactions?

How can you move toward the instructions of those verses? (Hint: read 2 Corinthians 3:5–6 and then ask God to work in your heart.)

Respond

Holy Father, please forgive me for all the times I've allowed sinful behavior to creep into my thoughts and conversations. I ask that You will now "search me, God, and know my heart; test me and know my anxious thoughts. See if there is any offensive way in me, and lead me in the way everlasting" (Ps. 139:23–24). Amen.

CHAPTER THIRTEEN: THE GREATNESS GAMES

Read and Reflect

Read Proverbs 21:21. To find life, prosperity, and honor, what two things do you need to pursue?

What do you think that looks like?

Read and Reflect

Read Ephesians 4. Write out verse 2 and then put the initials of a few people you need to apply this with. Pray for the Lord to help you … and pray for those people.

Write out any observations or instructions you needed to read today.

Respond

Lord, You are God. I am not. Forgive me for the times—the many, many times—when I invert this. Let me be found in You—in adoration of You, led by Your Spirit, washed in Your grace. Help me live for You today. Amen.

CHAPTER FOURTEEN: WHO ME? YEAH YOU! COULDN'T BE! THEN WHO?

Read and Reflect

Read 1 Chronicles 4:10. Jabez called upon the God of Israel, saying, "Oh that you would bless me and enlarge my border" (ESV). Consider the people in your life whom you influence. Write down at least five names. Pray for fresh vision, courage, and opportunities to make an impact in their lives for Christ.

Read and Reflect

Read Proverbs 16:3, which tells us to "commit to the LORD whatever you do, and he will establish your plans." Spend time in prayer and then write down some thoughts about what this verse can and should look like in your life.

Read and Reflect

Read Philippians 2:13. The apostle Paul brings some important reminders to us in this letter to the church of Philippi. Are you willing to yield to God's leading, to humble yourself before Him, and to allow God to work out His purpose in your life? Ask God to increase your desire to do these things and follow Him intimately.

Read and Reflect

Read Titus 2:3–5. List the behaviors that Paul encouraged older women to exhibit or refrain from.

What are some of the things Paul encouraged older women to teach younger women?

Respond

Lord, please keep my eyes open to opportunities to build others up in faith, and keep my heart firmly rooted in Your love so that I will always be prepared to give an answer for the reason of my hope. Help me remember that my moments are Your moments. Guide me as I plan each day and teach me to hold those plans loosely so that Your Spirit might lead every step. Thank You for impacting my life with Your grace and truth. Please open my eyes to see the opportunities all around me to point others to You. Stir my heart to make every day count for You. Amen.

ACKNOWLEDGMENTS

Brad, you are my rock and the biggest blessing in my life. Without you, there would be no *I Want It All*. Without you, I couldn't do what I do or dream the way I dream. You are my best friend, and I will always thank God for you. There's no one else I'd rather pursue God's heart with!

Huge hugs to my family for their constant support, prayers, and grace. My kids, my parents, my siblings, and my precious grandma—my heart is swollen with love and appreciation for all of you. And my friends! Tara, Susan, BJ, Sharon, Mary, April, Kim, and Josette … Karen and my prayer team … Kathi, my Weary Women Wednesday Skype sister … Jodie and Dinna. Goodness. Where in the world would I be without you guys? You are my people, and I am ridiculously honored by that little detail.

Massive love to the incredible team at David C Cook for the crazy awesome ways you have surrounded this book with support and professional excellence. Ingrid, thank you for believing in me and in this message. Chriscynethia and Marilyn—you two are amazing! Tim, not sure how or why, but you just get me. Scary, bro. But so much fun! Annette, Darren, and the rest of the marketing team, I have loved every moment of working with you. Lisa, my coffee and jewelry sister, thanks for rocking the publicity and just for your overall adorableness. Amy, thanks for being amazing with the cover and all things creative. Good glory, I just love you all!

Bill Jensen, you are an incredible agent and a delightful friend. Thank you for cheering me on and for being a sounding board over the years. Dave Clark, I am continually astounded and humbled that I get to work with you, write with you, dream with you, and razz you. What a journey!

Liz Heaney, you are more than just a best-in-the-business editor. You are an encourager, a teacher, a polisher, and a new friend. This book is better because of you. Thank you. Thank you. Thank you.

More than anything, I give thanks and honor and glory to my precious Jesus. I am blown away that You invited me to join You on this incredible pursuit of Your everything. My life will never be the same.

NOTES

CHAPTER 2

1. Strong's Exhaustive Concordance, s.v. G4492, "rooted"; Thayer's Greek Lexicon, s.v. "rhizoō," cited in BlueLetterBible.org, https://www.blueletterbible.org/lang/lexicon/lexicon.cfm?Strongs=G4492&t=KJV.

CHAPTER 3

1. William Arndt, Frederick W. Danker, and Walter Bauer, A Greek-English Lexicon of the New Testament and Other Early Christian Literature, 3rd ed. (Chicago: University of Chicago Press, 2000), 42.
2. Robert L. Thomas, New American Standard Hebrew-Aramaic and Greek Dictionaries, rev. ed (Anaheim, CA: Foundation Publications, 1998), s.v. "rapha."
3. Timothy Keller, Twitter quote, @DailyKeller, December 28, 2013.
4. Richard Sibbes, The Bruised Reed (Edinburgh, UK: Banner of Truth Trust, 1998), 13.

CHAPTER 4

1. Laurie Isop, How Do You Hug a Porcupine? (New York: Simon & Schuster, 2011).
2. Charles Swindoll, Growing Strong in the Seasons of Life (Grand Rapids, MI: Zondervan, 1983), 163.

CHAPTER 5

1. Strong's Exhaustive Concordance, s.v. H3045, "acknowledge," cited in BlueLetterBible.org, https://www.blueletterbible.org/lang/lexicon/lexicon.cfm?strongs=H3045.

2. *Pooh's Grand Adventure: The Search for Christopher Robin*, directed by Karl Geurs (Disney Television Animation, 1997).

CHAPTER 6

1. *Strong's Exhaustive Concordance*, s.v. G3875, "Helper," cited in BlueLetterBible.org, https://www.blueletterbible.org/lang/lexicon/lexicon.cfm?Strongs=G3875&t=ESV.

CHAPTER 8

1. Omnipoll, cited in "New Research Explores the Changing Shape of Temptation," Barna Group, January 4, 2013, https://www.barna.org/barna-update/culture/600 -new-years-resolutions-temptations-and-americas-favorite-sins#.VgVUDOlNs7d.

CHAPTER 9

1. Max Lucado, *Grace for the Moment: Inspirational Thoughts for Each Day of the Year* (Nashville: Thomas Nelson, 2000), 134.
2. Saint Augustine, *Confessions*, 1.1.1.

CHAPTER 10

1. M/A/R/R/S, "Pump Up the Volume," © 1987 4AD.
2. Paul Tournier, quoted in Phillip Yancey, *Disappointment with God: Three Questions No One Asks Aloud* (New York: HarperCollins, 1988), 244.
3. Mark Batterson, *The Circle Maker: Praying Circles around Your Biggest Dreams and Greatest Fears* (Grand Rapids: Zondervan, 2011), 122.

CHAPTER 13

1. Tony Evans, *Kingdom Man: Every Man's Destiny, Every Woman's Dream* (Carol Stream, IL: Tyndale, 2012), 40.
2. Nichole Nordeman, *Love Story: The Hand That Holds Us from the Garden to the Gates* (Brentwood, TN: Worthy Publishing, 2012), 75.

CHAPTER 14

1. John Acuff, "The Truth about Callings," *Stuff Christians Like* (blog), November 17, 2013, http://stuffchristianslike.net/2013/11/17/truth-callings/.

ABOUT THE AUTHOR

Gwen lives in the Queen City of Charlotte, North Carolina, but most days she refrains from wearing a tiara. Gwen and her husband, Brad, have been married since 1993 and are parents to three tall teens who keep them on their toes and on their knees. The Smiths stay busy by frequenting various volleyball and basketball courts in the greater Carolina region and by serving in their local church, LIFE Fellowship.

Gwen is the author of several books, a gifted songwriter, and a sought-after speaker and worship leader. Gwen is also the cofounder of Girlfriends in God, a conference and devotional ministry.

Connect with Gwen:
Website: www.GwenSmith.net
Facebook: www.facebook.com/GwenSmithMusic
Twitter, Instagram, and Pinterest: @GwenSmithMusic

For more book-related resources:
www.IWantItAllBook.com
#iwantitall